Football for Moms and Sweethearts

by

John Paul Garner

FOOTBALL FOR MOMS AND SWEETHEARTS
Copyright © 2011 John Paul Garner
All rights reserved.

Published by Create Space 2017
North Charleston, South Carolina, USA

No parts of this publication may be reproduced, stored in a retrieval system, or transmitted in any form or by any means, electronic, mechanical, photocopying, recording, or otherwise, without the prior written permission of the copyright owner.

This book is sold subject to the condition that it shall not, by way of trade or otherwise, be lent, resold, hired out, or otherwise circulated without the publisher's prior consent in any form of binding or cover other than that in which it is published and without a similar condition including this condition being imposed on the subsequent purchaser. Under no circumstances may any part of this book be photocopied for resale.

Cover Art from Google Images
Back Cover Photography:
- The One Mom (Kathy Sunderman)
- The Two Moms (Carlton Holls)
- The College Student (One Raised Eyebrow)

Library of Congress Control Number: 2017910735

For Gigi and Devyn.

The two humans I love most.

And then there's our four dogs.

I love them too.

What's Inside...

Moms is organized into sections that explain a specific aspect of the game. At the backend of most sections is a slice of football history or of something technical that will either add to your love of the game or to your understanding of it. In the content listing below, those slices are italicized.

Often you'll encounter an illustration that will help you understand a particular concept. The illustrations are fairly standard to what coaches draw up on a whiteboard. The ovals are offensive players, and the letters are abbreviations for a position on the defensive side of the ball. The rectangle among the ovals is the center—the guy who snaps the ball to get an offensive play started. The defense will always be on top, and the offense opposite it, at the bottom.

In the Beginning...	1
Offense	
Football's First Modern Offense	2
Formations	3
Football's Chicken Bone	5
Shifts and Motion	
The Jet Sweep and the Reverse	6
Offensive Line	7
The Battles at the Line	8
Quarterback	11
The Pre-Snap Read	12
Running Back	13
The Elmira Express	14
Receiver	16
Selling the Nine	17
The Run Play	
Football's Most Dangerous Play	18
The Pass Play	20
It Was Leif, Not Chris	21
Trickeration	23
The Tackle Eligible	
Play Calling	24
Where "Downs" Come From?	
The New Math	25
Identifying Offenses	26
The Lonesome Polecat	27
Defense	29
The Okie	
Defensive Line	30
Techniques	31
Linebacker	32
Football's Toughest Tackle	34
Defensive Back	35
One- and Two-High Safeties	36
Defending the Run	37
A Hat in the Crack	38
Defending the Pass	
Tampa Two	39
Blitzing and Stunting	40
Zone Dog	41
Identifying Defenses	42
The Top Two Defenses	
Special Teams	43
Swinging Gate	46
Scoring	
Time	47
The Field and Its Features	49
A Brief History of Hashmarks	50
What's a Gridiron?	51
Player Numbers	
Scoreboard	
Chain Crew	52
Common Rule Violations	
Common TV Terms	55
Football's Coldest Game	66
The President Who Saved Football	71
Football's Basic Pass Defenses	73
Some Food For Thought	78

FOOTBALL FOR MOMS AND SWEETHEARTS

(Rutgers Athletics)

Football is played on a rectangular field 120 yards long and 53-1/3 yards wide, between two teams consisting of 11 players each. The team in possession of the ball is called the offense, and the team opposing it—the defense.

The object of the game is for one team to score more points than their opponent. The offense seeks to score, and the defense seeks to prevent it. Scoring occurs when the ball is carried into the end zone or is kicked through the goalposts at the back of each end zone.

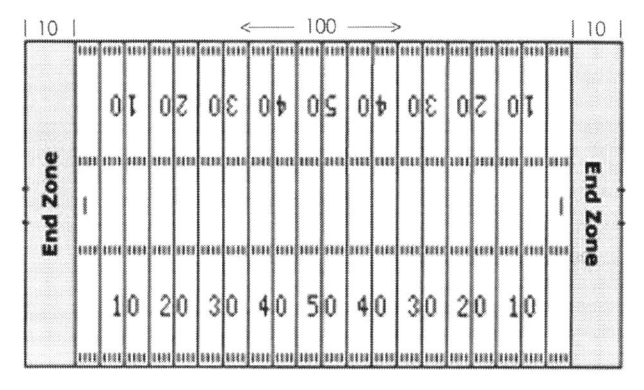

The ball is advanced across the field, either by running it or throwing it—what is called a *pass*. Each attempt to advance the ball is called a *play*. The offense is given four plays—or *downs*, as you'll often hear TV commentators refer to them—to advance the ball at least ten yards to be awarded another series of four downs.

If, during the four downs, the offense fails to gain the yardage needed to earn a first down, it must surrender possession of the ball to the opposing team. It generally does so on fourth down by kicking the ball to the defense—what is called a *punt*.

It's the strategies an offense uses to advance the ball during its four downs, versus the tactics the defense uses to stop it, that make football so exciting and so popular. And it is the speed of the players that determines how sophisticated the schemes are that offenses and defenses use in a game. The higher the level of competition, the faster the players are, and the more artful the game is.

In the Beginning . . .

. . . there was something resembling soccer. That's the game that was played on November 6, 1869, when Rutgers and its close neighbor Princeton are credited with having played the first game of football. Rutgers won, 6-4. And yes, technically, the game was football. But not the football we know and love, and what we now watch with great enthusiasm, which was actually fashioned from the rough and tumble of rugby.

That came about in 1874 when McGill University in Montreal looked southward and challenged Harvard to two games: one a game using Harvard's soccer rules, and the other a game of rugby. Harvard liked the rugby-style game—which ended in a scoreless tie—because the players got to run with the ball and other players got to tackle them. You know, like football. So shortly afterward, Harvard started challenging other American colleges to rugby matches.

(College Sports Report)

The rugby-style game soon became the favorite among the eastern colleges. Later, a visionary coach from Yale named Walter Camp devised new rules that standardized the game and, when coupled with the acceptance of the forward pass in 1906, set football on a path to become the game we watch today.

OFFENSE

FOOTBALL FOR MOMS AND SWEETHEARTS

The goal of an offense is to score by carrying the ball into the opponent's *end zone* as often as possible, either by running or throwing.

Basically, an offense is comprised of four positions: *quarterback*, *running back*, *receiver*, and *offensive lineman*. The quarterback, running back(s), and receivers are considered the skill positions because of the unique athletic abilities they routinely display in performing their assignments.

They're really good, especially in the pros.

Typical Offensive Formation

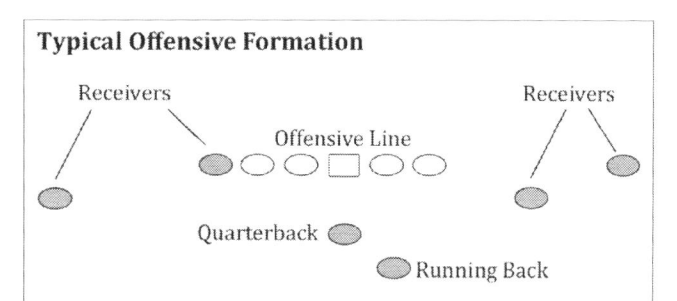

Receivers — Receivers
Offensive Line
Quarterback
Running Back

NOTE: No matter how the players are arranged in a formation, for it to be legal, it must have at least seven players on the line of scrimmage.

Offensive linemen, on the other hand, are the blue-collar workers. They do the dirty work. It's often the most important work, and they do it with great pride and skill. They are routinely overlooked, but all coaches know that no offense—or team—can succeed without them.

Offensive Line

(SD Kirk)

What an offense does to advance the ball to make a first down or score, be it a run or pass play, will routinely depend upon how the coaches think they can attack a defense and where in their study of an opponent's game film they have detected a weakness or a tendency in the tactics a defense will use in certain situations. That information forms the basis for the offensive game plan and is often charted by down and distance. (*See Play Calling*)

There are basically three offensive philosophies: control the football versus a balanced approach versus score, score, score. The first tactic—*ball control*—is slow-paced and methodical. Basically, it is a pound-the-rock approach, which is coachspeak for running the ball. It's goal is to eat-up-the-clock and keep the other team's offense on the sideline. If it's on the sideline, it isn't scoring.

The second approach—the balanced attack—is a measured mix of run and pass, while the third philosophy—the *no-huddle, uptempo* attack—is about speed. Fast to assemble at the line, fast to call a play, fast to execute that play, and fast to score. Real fast.

Where the ball control team will use the 25 or 40 seconds allotted it to organize a play, the uptempo offense wants to line up and go in under 15 seconds. *Fifteen seconds!* Some want to go faster—and some do.

As the uptempo team assembles at the line, it may seem like you're watching a fire drill at times, but at that rate, the uptempo team can run, on average, about 90 plays a game, while the ball control team will average around 60.

The difference does two things that creates a distinct advantage for the uptempo offense: it's 30 more plays that an opponent's defense is on the field, getting tired and maybe making mistakes, and it's 30 more chances to score

All three philosophies work, and all three have their merits, but it's clear that the most exciting to watch is the uptempo offense. Just as an opposing defense doesn't get a chance to catch it's breath trying to stop it, neither do the fans trying to watch it.

FOOTBALL'S FIRST MODERN OFFENSE

The man best known for the rule changes to the game of rugby that started its evolution into the game we know today is also the man who first toyed with the formation that, in the hands of Clark Shaughnessy, became football's first modern offense: the "T."

FOOTBALL FOR MOMS AND SWEETHEARTS

Back in the 1880s when Walter Camp, later acknowledged as the Father of American Football, played with the T, he called it the "regular" formation. It can be found in some vintage playbooks, but it never rose to prominence until around 1940 when Shaughnessy, married it to the gifted athletes he inherited at Stanford University.

Regular Formation

(J. Lyndon)

Pop Warner—the godfather of football coaches back then, who was most noted for inventing the heavy-handed single and double-wing offenses that had dominated the game for decades—was reported to have predicted that Stanford wouldn't win a single game using that "crazy" formation. Going so far as to call it "ridiculous."

To Coach Warner's chagrin and possible embarrassment, the Cardinal went on to an undefeated season and a Rose Bowl victory using what most coaches at the time thought was a "gadget" offense.

"T" Formation
Chicago Bears - 1943
(Youtube)

It took a forward thinker like George Halas to see its potential. The venerable head coach of the Chicago Bears took notice of Stanford's success that year and asked Shaughnessy to help prepare his Bears for the NFL championship game that year.

Their opponent was the Washington Redskins, who had defeated the Bears three weeks earlier, 7-3. The win made them a sight favorite. They even boasted publicly about how the Bears had quit during the game.

Using Shaughnessy's brilliant game plan, the Bear's—scoring on a 68-yard run on the second play of the game —routed the Redskins, 73-0. The score is still the most lopsided in NFL history. Ten years later the "T" had replaced Pop Warner's low-scoring and boring offenses at most of the colleges and pro teams in the country because of what that "crazy" offense did in that one game in 1940.

Shaughnessy introduced several innovative ideas to the game—like putting a man in motion—but the thing that made the T rock was positioning the quarterback under the center, from where he received the snap, executed hand-offs or fakes, or dropped back to pass.

(Wikipedia)

Unlike what the quarterback did in Pop Warner's dinosaur systems, where he was primarily a blocking back, the quarterback in the T became the focal point of the offense. Its leader.

Modern quarterbacks like Tom Brady, Aaron Rogers, or Matt Ryan need to burn candles in Clark Shaughnessy's name because it's for sure that none of them would last very long in the NFL if the single wing had survived and they had to block for a living.

But the most important thing the T did, besides revolutionize the game, was make football fun to watch. The T was a crowd pleaser. It's blend of run plays and run fakes that, because the ball had been reduced in size, led to precision passing, lots of scoring, and packed stadiums everywhere. Because of the T, the game took on a new life, a new look, and a new level of excitement.

FORMATIONS

How the offense arranges its players at the line of scrimmage to start a play is called a "formation." No matter how a formation looks, seven of its 11 players must always be on the line of scrimmage. Seven!

The seven generally consist of five offensive linemen—the big guys—and two players positioned at either end of the line. They can be tight to the offensive line, or split wide. They are receivers. While there can be more than seven players on the line, there can't be less, or it's an illegal formation.

So, if there are seven on the line, that leaves four players to form what is commonly called the *offensive backfield* behind the offensive line. All four of them are eligible receivers as well, except in the NFL where quarterbacks can not go out for a pass.

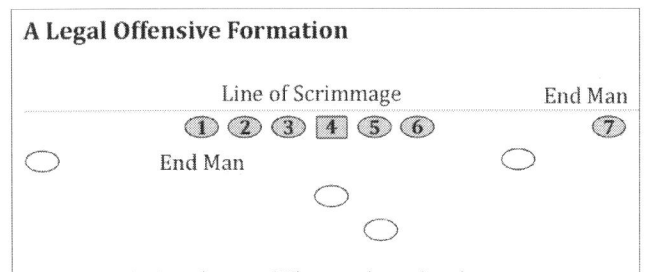

A Legal Offensive Formation

```
                 Line of Scrimmage          End Man
                 ① ② ③ ④ ⑤ ⑥                ⑦
         ○                            ○
              End Man
                          ○
                            ○
```

NOTE: Again it makes no difference how the players are arranged in a formation, so long as there are at least seven of them at the line of scrimmage. The four behind them are considered to be in the offensive backfield.

How a formation looks is often a clue to the offense's intent. For example, "spread" formations do exactly that, they "spread" or stretch a defense from sideline to sideline, creating space—what coaches call "open grass"—for the offense to attack.

Spread

(Brent Flanders)

Heavy or jumbo formations—which compact a defense—often seek to outnumber and overpower it at the point of attack or deceive it as to the direction of the attack.

Heavy Formation

(Carl Burgchardt)

But given how often you'll see the football passed, another strategy seen in the design of a formation is to create a physical mismatch between a receiver and the defender assigned to him. The formation might match a tall receiver to a short defender or—even scarier for the defense—a fast receiver to a slower defender.

The thing to remember is that every formation must conform to two rules: the seven-men-on-the-line rule discussed previously and the rule governing "eligible" receivers. Those are the guys who can run past the line of scrimmage and catch a pass. To understand how that works, let's do a little math.

In any offensive play, there are six players of the 11 on the field who are eligible to go beyond the line of scrimmage and catch a pass: the four players lined up in the backfield—which includes the quarterback except in the pros—and the two players lined up at either end of the offensive formation, as diagrammed below.

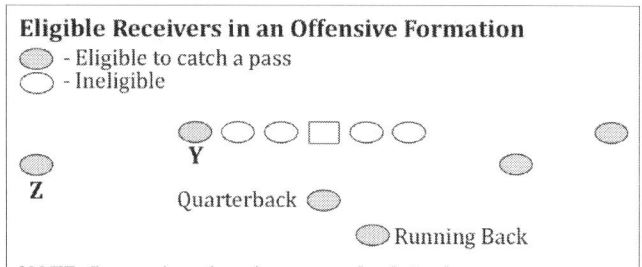

Eligible Receivers in an Offensive Formation

● - Eligible to catch a pass
○ - Ineligible

```
              ● ○ ○ □ ○ ○              ●
                  Y
         ●                         ○
         Z       Quarterback ○
                               ● Running Back
```

NOTE: Remember that the quarterback in the pros can not go out for a pass. Also only the end man on the line is an eligible receiver, which is why the flanker (Z) does not cover the tight end (Y).

But only five of the six players can go out for a pass because of the 11 players on the offensive team, the five offensive linemen must block for the one who throws the ball—usually the quarterback—leaving five players who can catch a pass.

Within those constraints, an offensive coordinator —the coach who designs the offense and "calls" the plays in a game—is limited only by his imagination and the physical skills of his players as to the variety of formations he can conjure up to outstrategize his counterpart: the defensive coordinator.

But whatever formation an offense uses, be it a spread, a heavy, or even a balanced look that positions an even number of players on either side of the center, you can be sure that its purpose is to create an advantage for the offense.

The thing to remember is that whatever advantage a formation creates for an offense, it's the defense's job to counter it.

FOOTBALL'S CHICKEN BONE

When first revealed to the public during a game against Houston on September 21, 1968, the Texas offense that was part power and part slight of hand was a disappointment. It didn't even have a name.

And while that would come later, that debut game ended in a tie, and the offense—a descendant of the Split-T system that head coach Darrell Royal had run as a quarterback at Oklahoma, but which was mostly the brainchild of assistant coach Emory Bellard—was heavily criticized by Longhorn fans and the Texas media alike.

Nobody liked it—especially after Texas lost its second game using the new-fangled offense. The reason was that almost nobody understood it. Nobody, that is, except Emory Bellard, the brainiac who had conjured it up on a blackboard.

It wasn't until Texas played arch-rival Oklahoma in its annual battle at the Cotton Bowl, and only after James Street guided the offense on a masterful, field-long drive to win the game in the fourth quarter, that Ballard's version of a triple-threat, option attack was received as a legitimate work of art and less the work of idiots.

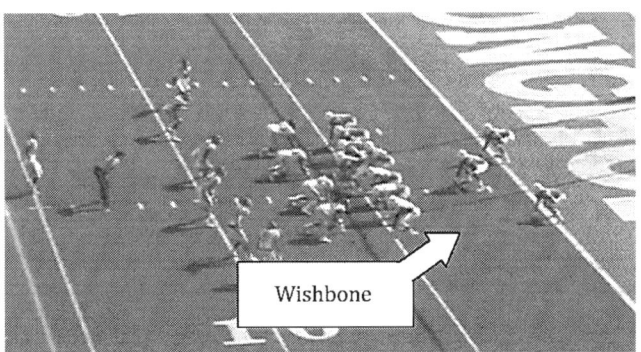

Wishbone

(YouTube)

The offense was dubbed the "Wishbone," not by its inventor but rather by a sportswriter because the curious "Y" arrangement of the running backs in the backfield reminded him of that peculiar part of a chicken. Texas would win its next 30 games and two National Championships using that mystical chicken bone system.

Later, in the hands of Barry Switzer and the Oklahoma Sooners, the Wishbone would achieve even greater success and become the dominant offense in college football during the '70s and early '80s. Its slide from prominence came with the rise of an even more unconventional attack called the "spread."

But its descendant, the "Flexbone," is active today. Georgia Tech uses the newer version of the triple-option attack with great success, as do the service academies—Navy, Army, and Air Force. They like that the offense is an equalizer because of their size limitations, that is, the size of the athletes they can recruit and put on the field.

It's also popular because it's extremely difficult for opponents to prepare for in one week. More so than the uptempo spread attacks they will see.

Flexbone

(Henry deSaussure Copeland)

There's a kind of poetic justice that, in a football landscape dotted with big-money programs using pass-happy spread systems, the academies—who are a natural fit for the Flexbone offense because of their discipline, traditions and academics—routinely beat bigger schools and their bigger players using an option attack that was imagined while its creator was watching a basketball game in 1941.

SHIFTS AND MOTION

Another way that offenses can increase their advantage is to try to confuse a defense by *shifting* personnel or sending a player in *motion*. Once the offense is formed at the line of scrimmage and set for one second—meaning motionless—it's allowed to shift anyone except the offensive linemen, who have their "hand in the ground." This is called a 3-point stance.

(Thought.com)

A *shift* is when designated "skill" players move from one position to another in the formation prior to the snap, while *motion* is when one player in the backfield, meaning "off the line," starts running towards the formation, or away from it, but never towards the line of scrimmage until the ball is snapped. These changes to the formation are called "pre-snap movements," and each can create a distinct advantage for the offense.

(Ken Lund)

Motion is the pre-snap movement you will most often see. Its most common purposes are:

- Change the formation strength by gaining a numbers advantage,
- Determine the kind of pass defense the defense is using,
- Ease a speedy receiver's quick release into a pass route,
- Disguise an offense's intentions,
- Compel an opponent to waste practice time preparing for it,
- Create a mismatch in skill with a particular defensive player.

Formation shifts can achieve the same tactical goals as motion, but they also force a defense to quickly adjust their plan of attack, which can cause confusion and hesitation among its players, especially when the defense has not seen the shifts on film and not "game planned" for them.

To execute a shift or send a man in motion, an offense must be "set"—meaning motionless—for one count of the snapcount before the change can occur. Only one player can go in motion, and as we mentioned, he can make no move toward the line of scrimmage until the ball is snapped.

If both a shift and motion have been called, the shift occurs first, followed by the motion. In between the two the offense must again be set for one count. There's an old adage in football that says, "If you're thinkin', you're stinkin'!" So with this in mind, the basic objective of motion and shifting is to get a defense to think—and not react—which makes them slower and easier to attack.

THE JET SWEEP AND THE REVERSE

(Hero Sports)

Amos Alonzo Stagg is credited with developing it. Clark Shaughnessy is noted for putting it to good use in his T-formation offense which catapulted pro football into the modern era. And Sid Luckman, a quarterback for the Chicago Bears back in the '40s, once wrote that the "several hundred plays" contained in his playbook "... gave him over 1,000 options for man-in-motion deceptions."

FOOTBALL FOR MOMS AND SWEETHEARTS

One thousand? Who can remember that many plays? But if true, it gives credence to the value a man in motion can have to an offensive attack.

As you learned in the previous section, a man in motion can add to an offense's understanding of the defensive scheme. But where you'll see spread teams use a man in motion most often is in a run play that has its roots in the Wing-T offenses of the 1950s.

Back then it was called a "Fly Sweep." Now that we have faster modes of travel, it's called the "Jet Sweep." Jet because it's fast, and sweep because, like all sweep plays, it attacks where a defense is weakest: outside.

What it isn't, is a reverse.

A reverse starts out in one direction to get the defense flowing, or at least leaning in that direction then, after a hand-off, attacks in the opposite direction. It's a great way to attack a defense that's overpursuing.

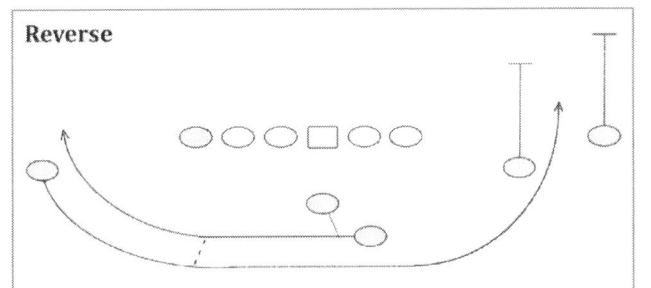

Reverse

NOTE: A reverse can start with a hand-off to a running back who runs toward the outside, drawing the defense. He then hands-off or laterals to a receiver going in the opposite direction.

The jet sweep, meanwhile, is a nitro-fueled race down a quarter-mile track. Most often, because of his speed, it starts with motion from a wide receiver positioned outside the formation who races towards the offensive backfield. The supersonic speed of the motion is a clue that what's coming is a jet sweep.

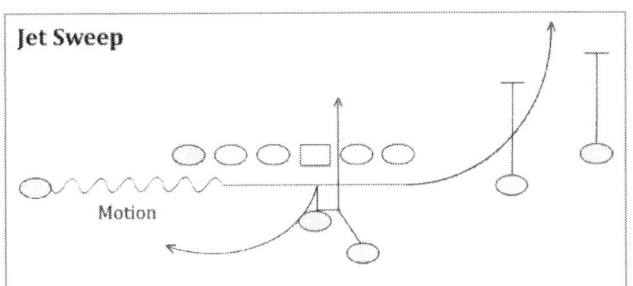

Jet Sweep

Motion

NOTE: The ballcarrier races toward the quarterback who fakes a hand-off into the line, then hands-off to the sweeper. The sweeper never slows down and races around the end.

Once in the backfield, the receiver doesn't slowdown to accept a well-timed hand-off from the quarterback, but looking like he's been shot out of the starship Enterprise, he continues past the edge of the formation and into the defense's perimeter. It's one continuous motion.

But where it might be confused with a reverse is in the design of some jet sweeps that have the quarterback faking a hand-off to a running back in the backfield before he hands off to the receiver coming from outside the formation. The fake—like in a reverse—gets the defense to lean in the wrong direction or freeze long enough to allow the jet sweep to develop after the hand-off.

Deception is employed in both plays. A fake into the line in the jet sweep and an attack in the opposite direction in the reverse. Deception is the thing that makes the reverse work, while speed is the key component of the jet sweep.

But once you see both in action and become familiar with each, you'll see for yourself that the jet sweep is not a reverse. It's actually more like an endaround, *in which an "end"—the old school term for a receiver—runs from one side of a formation "around" to the other.*

OFFENSIVE LINE

(Mark Briscoe)

The "big uglies." They do one thing: they block. They're not, however, the offensive players who get the most attention from fans and the media. Those are the guys who handle the ball. The guys who run with it, catch it, or throw it. They're the glamour guys. The celebrities. But they're not the most important guys. That distinction belongs to the offensive line—the guys up front.

FOOTBALL FOR MOMS AND SWEETHEARTS

Offensive linemen are the biggest offensive players, so it's hard to miss them, yet their play often goes unnoticed. There are five of them: a center who is, as his name suggests, positioned in the center of the line with a guard on either side of him, and a tackle outside the guards. If you hear their jersey number called out, chances are its because they have committed an infraction of the rules.

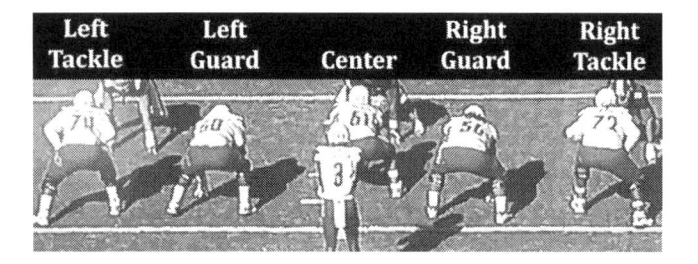

[Image: Offensive line positions labeled Left Tackle, Left Guard, Center, Right Guard, Right Tackle]

But if you want to quickly know what the play is, the offensive line is the first place to look. It's what the defense does. Because if it's a run play, the offensive line is firing across the line of scrimmage and engaging defenders.

But if it's a pass play, they're setting up at the line to pass block—or "high hatting" as it's often referred to—because their pad level is elevated when they pass block, while it's low when they run block. The offensive tackles, in fact, are retreating because the defenders coming off the edge are coming hard and fast.

[Image labeled "High Hat"]

(Rick Elliot)

It used to be that the offensive guards were the most active linemen in that they'd "pull" from their position on the line and block elsewhere, "kicking out" an edge defender or "trapping" an aggressive defensive lineman. They still do, but they're not the only guys who pull anymore.

Nowadays, the offensive tackles and even the center pull, which is an indication of the great athletic abilities these very large men possess. Of these skills the most important is "good feet."

When a college line coach evaluates video of a high school prospect, the two things he looks for first are the player's footwork and does he finish the play—does he block to the whistle? The one, good feet, translates into speed and leverage—which is the simple physics of being in the right position to move an object. In this case, a defender.

Good footwork makes that happen—and makes it happen fast. Technique, as one NFL lineman explained, can be taught, but speed—or "smooth" feet—can not.

The other, finishing a play, is about attitude, because no task on the football field is harder than blocking at the line of scrimmage. It's not simply skill that makes an offensive lineman good—or great—at his job, but the level of focus and dedication he applies to the task. Something known simply as heart, especially in an uptempo offense that averages 90 plays per game.

The thing to remember about the offense is that no run or pass play will advance the ball if the offensive line isn't doing its job. That job is to block, and that's all they do. They're either attacking defenders and moving them out of the way during a run play, or they're shielding the quarterback from defenders during a pass play.

So while offensive linemen might be the "big uglies" and toil in obscurity, what they do and how they do it is a thing of beauty when it's working. And the way you can tell it's working—that what you're watching is a masterpiece—is that the offense is moving the ball and scoring.

THE BATTLES AT THE LINE

Football is conflict. This conflict is no more evident—or violent—than in the battles along the line of scrimmage where strength and positioning—what coaches call "leverage"—often determine the winner. Here among the down linemen—the guys in 2- and 3-point stances—there are no Davids. There are only Goliaths.

FOOTBALL FOR MOMS AND SWEETHEARTS

(Hector Alejandro)

That which separates the combatants is a no-man's land. It is a swath of turf called the neutral zone. No one except the offensive center can intrude upon this sacred ground and him only because he must handle the ball to snap it.

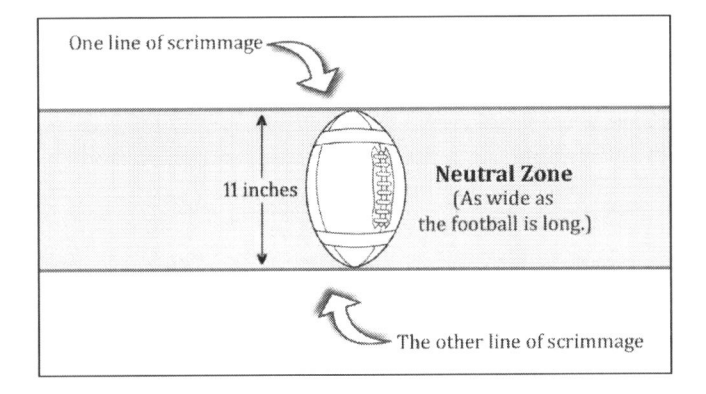

In terms of dimensions, it is as wide as a football is long: about 11 inches. Each tip of the football is a coordinate in separate lines of scrimmage that stretch from sideline to sideline: one for the defense and one for the offense.

"Moving the sticks"—that is to say, to make first downs and move the ball towards an opponent's end zone—involves three forms of attack: running the ball, the play-action pass, which is a pass play that starts out looking like a run play, and passing the ball. Of the three strategies, the run is universally considered the most important. It sets up everything else. And when successful it is the best way to demoralize an opponent.

For starters, if an offense can run the ball, defensive linemen can't tee off and rush the passer. They must "play" the run first. Secondly, the defense must play closer to the line and load the box—that is, position more players closer to the offensive line to stop the run which, in turn, opens the back end of the field to an attack from the pass.

The offensive line must move or "drive" the defensive line backward off the line of scrimmage or "off the ball." If they can do that consistently, they will dominate the line of scrimmage and the offense can then run the ball, leading to a balanced offense between all three forms of attack.

But if they can't get any push, the offense will have difficulty integrating the play-action pass into its attack. As a result it will be forced to rely almost exclusively on the pass, which will make it one-dimensional and easy to defend. Even the pass-happy offenses of the no-huddle variety must run the ball once in a while, and do so successfully.

Defenses, meanwhile, are trained to stop the run. For the defensive lineman, the key to winning his individual battle is to get off the block of the offensive lineman. The faster he can throw his hands into his counterpart, the more force he will generate, and for him, force translates into control.

While an offensive lineman wants to engage and drive a defender "off the ball," a defensive lineman doesn't want to be moved and in his initial charge he will either attempt to escape the offensive lineman's attempt to block him or he will "stalemate" him. That is to say neutralize him so that there is no movement off the line of scrimmage.

(Rick Elliot)

The offensive line will engage the defense or "fire out" on the snapcount, which is the signal the quarterback calls for the ball to be snapped and put into play. To move defenders or prevent their penetration into the backfield, the offensive line will use a variety of blocking techniques and schemes.

In a running play, the types of blocks most often used are the drive block, which is a one-on-one, man-on-man block; the double team, where two offensive linemen work together to crush a defender; or the zone block, in which offensive linemen work in tandem to block whoever shows up in their area of responsibility.

(Ben Ostrander – www.benostrander.com)

Pass blocking, however, is entirely different from run blocking. Instead of attacking a defender and moving him, the offensive lineman is basically catching and channeling him away from the quarterback, who is setting up in the backfield, looking to throw the ball.

Often, pass protection, when performed as designed, will look like a semi-circle or cup—what is routinely called a "pass pocket". A defensive lineman, meanwhile, attacks on the movement of the ball. He shouldn't be listening to the quarterback call his signals or he might—and sometimes does—jump into offsides because of it.

(Thomas L. Cox)

Prior to the snap, he is focusing on some part of the offensive lineman opposite him—probably the "V" in the neck—so that at the snap he can quickly analyze if the play is a pass or run. If the offensive lineman's helmet or "hat" stays low at the snap and he fires out, the play is most likely a run. If it rises and he retreats, then it is generally a pass play.

To shut down the run, defenses assign a defender to each gap created by an offensive formation. Each defender is then responsible for protecting his assigned area from attack by the offense. This is called "gap integrity" or "gap control." To maintain gap discipline, defensive linemen will either "read and react" or "read on the run."

"Read" means analyze. In the one scheme, a defensive lineman analyzes the play while engaging an offensive lineman. He then reacts to it by shedding the blocker and pursuing the ball.

In a read-and-react scheme, the defensive linemen are generally lined up on an offensive lineman or "heads up." This is because they are routinely responsible for the gaps on either side of the lineman over which they are aligned.

Whereas, in a read-on-the-run scheme, the D-linemen are off-set in what is called a "shade" alignment. This allows them to attack and penetrate their assigned gap much quicker. In the other scheme, he analyzes the play while he's attacking a gap. His goal is to penetrate the offensive backfield and put immediate pressure on the offense. The differences between these two philosophies will usually determine where a defensive lineman lines up and how he plays his position.

A Hat in the Crack.

(Curt Hart)

FOOTBALL FOR MOMS AND SWEETHEARTS

The tactics a defensive line can use to attack an offense will often include stunting. A stunt—or "game" as some coaches call it—generally involves two or more defenders who line up in one position then, at the snap of the ball, attack someplace else.

Essentially, what the defenders involved in a stunt do is trade assignments so as to confuse the offensive line and disrupt its blocking scheme. While these tactics are expected, and countermeasures are developed to stop them, they nonetheless add to the great difficulty of playing offensive line. (See Blitzes and Stunts)

Though the battles along the line of scrimmage are routinely described as war, and its participants as combatants, we rarely watch the action between the opposing linemen. On a stage 100 yards long and 53 yards wide, it is the more visible and more glamorous running backs and receivers who receive our attentions and are elevated to star status.

But coaches and players both know that the true heroes—the real warriors—are found in the length of a football, in the 11 inches of turf that separate the offensive line from the defensive line. It is there, in what has been called the "trenches" where the most violent struggles occur; where the strongest and the swiftest prevail.

In those duels between titans, it is the player who has leverage—who is in a better position to move his opponent—that usually prevail. And it is the linemen who win most of the battles that determines the outcome of a game. For if any constant emerges from football's elegant geometry and simple physics, it's that the team who controls the line of scrimmage is the team that wins.

QUARTERBACK

The quarterback is the player directing the offense, sort of like the conductor of an orchestra. He's the player aligned directly behind the center, either up under him or in a shotgun position. He's the one barking out signals and maybe changing the play, the one who receives the snap—when the ball is hiked—and the one who hands the ball off, throws it, or runs it himself.

He's the leader of the offense. The field general. How he commands a huddle—when the offensive players gather together to learn what play they will execute and the signal at which the ball will be hiked—will often determine the outcome of a game, particularly in critical situations.

(Carlton Holls)

Quarterbacks are routinely selected for their physical skills and how they fit into a team's offensive system. For example, an offense built on passing the ball will want a quarterback who can make all the throws and do so accurately. On the other hand, an offense built on running the ball, like an option offense, will want a player who has quick feet and can make quick decisions in tight spaces.

Pocket presence is another trait sought in a quarterback, most especially in an offense that favors the pass. It's like a sixth sense, a kind of radar, that alerts the quarterback to the nearness of a pass rush that, like incoming missiles, comes at him at supersonic speeds and from different directions.

You'll see it in the way the quarterback steps up in the pocket to avoid the grasp of a defender, or slides to the side, or nimbly spins out of the pocket. Simply put, pocket presence is the ability to sense pressure and to escape it.

But there are intangibles as well. Intelligence is one. "Football IQ" coaches call it. Does the player understand the geometry of the game? Can he determine a defense's intent by analyzing—what coaches call "reading"—its alignment, where and how certain players are positioned. Can he check out of a bad play call and into a good one that attacks the defense where it's weakest in the 25 seconds an offense has to snap the ball?

FOOTBALL FOR MOMS AND SWEETHEARTS

Toughness is another intangible, and maybe the most important. It's critical to any position but most especially the quarterback because all eyes are on him. Playing quarterback is not for prima donnas. Defenders are always looking to deliver a hit.

Standing in the pocket and delivering a pass downfield when defenders are inches from blowing him up, when his every instinct is telling him to run, takes toughness. To do it once, even twice, is impressive. To do it repeatedly, though, takes guts. That kind of toughness can inspire a team. It's the kind of toughness that teams rally around.

In the military, leaders are expected to lead by example. So too in football. Great quarterbacks are great leaders. They do more than just throw the ball accurately or run fast. Their attitude, their personality, how they play the game can elevate a team. There's a very small percentage of quarterbacks, especially in the pros, who can do that. Which is why those kinds of quarterbacks are sought after and, when found, get the big bucks.

(Thomas Grimm)

THE PRE-SNAP READ

What's with all the pointing and helmet-tapping and moving of players the quarterback does before the ball is snapped? How about the code words he barks out? What are they? What do they mean?

Peyton Manning is famous for being among football's best quarterbacks ever, but he's also noted for one word in particular that he often called out to his offense just before the ball was snapped. "Omaha! Omaha!" he could be heard yelling.

Omaha?

(Econo Auto Sales)

For the longest time, fans wondered what it meant. Finally, years later, the meaning of the mystery word was revealed. Reportedly, Omaha meant "opposite". Yeah, that's it. Opposite. It was a code word that changed the direction of a play.

If the play was going to the right, "Omaha" changed it to the left. And vice versa. What Peyton was doing was calling an "audible." He was changing the play at the line of scrimmage, based on his analysis of the defense, what is called a "pre-snap read."

There's a kind of science to a pre-snap read or at least a script or routine a quarterback follows to decipher a defense's intentions. He does that mostly by analyzing the position of certain players. There's no standard way to perform a pre-snap read.

Offensive coordinators have different methods, and so do different quarterbacks. Much of what they do in the seconds before the ball is snapped is based on their experience, their film study of the opponent, and the offensive system they're in.

Almost always the pre-snap read begins as the quarterback is walking to the line. Or, if he's in a shotgun position, as the offense is deploying. In all cases the pre-snap read involves some basic math and often starts deep, where the safeties are routinely positioned at the top of a defense. Their number tells him what to look for next. For example, if there's none, then he's likely going to see man coverage underneath and a blitz.

When a defense has no one deep, they're betting the rush can get to the quarterback before he can throw to an open receiver. Or, if it's a run play, before the ballcarrier can get started.

12

FOOTBALL FOR MOMS AND SWEETHEARTS

One or two safeties positioned deep will also lead him to certain conclusions about the scheme the defense is using, but he will need to confirm his analysis by looking at the position of other defenders. He can either continue his read with a look at the defenders outside the box, or he can count the number of defenders in the box.

(BJ Smith)

If he looks to the outside, he'll look at the defenders' alignment and their depth, how closely they're aligned to his receivers, or how far off. And by alignment, he's checking who they're looking at: him or the receiver. Either one can tell him the type of coverage they're using. If him, they're playing zone. If the receiver, they're in man coverage.

When he scans the defenders positioned in the box, he's counting their number. If there are six or more, there's a good chance someone is going to blitz. There's an even better chance that they're looking to shutdown any run play. It depends on the down-and-distance situation, how many yards the offense needs to gain a first down. Long yardage could mean the defense is anticipating a pass, so they'll blitz. But short yardage could mean they're looking for a run play.

No one aspect of a defense can reveal a defense's plan to a quarterback. It's a combination of things like that discussed above which is—to use Donald Trump's favorite word—a "very" general description of the process. There are so many other factors that go into a quarterback's pre-snap read of a defense. The thing to know is that the quarterback is trying to determine what will work and what won't, and if it won't work, what can he change to that will.

If the play called is a pass play, the quarterback is also prioritizing his post-snap read—what or who he's going to look at first, after the ball has been snapped. He has to know where to look first, then second—what is called his progression—because, in a best case scenario, he has at most three seconds to find and throw to an open receiver. Three seconds!

That is, surprisingly, a lot of time. Few offensive linemen can hold a block that long. Of the things a quarterback must do well, the pre-snap read just might be the most critical to an offense's success or failure.

Because, when to call "Omaha! Omaha!" can easily be the difference between winning and losing.

RUNNING BACK

Running backs carry "the rock." That is, they run with the ball. And when they're not "creasing" a defense, they can block for whoever is. Or they can come out of the backfield and catch passes. But primarily, they carry the rock.

(RC Denton High School)

There are the fast and quick backs, and there are power backs. They're the "ooh and ah" guys who produce the spectacular runs. Fast backs slice through a defense and operate with skill in space. They can stretch a defense, penetrating deep into it and beyond it to the end zone.

(Ed Yourdon)

13

Quick backs can "break ankles," as coaches say, because they're so shifty and elusive, while power backs break tackles and get some YAC. That's an acronym unique to football that translates into "Yards After Contact." (Note: YAC can also mean "Yards After Catch" if describing a receiver.)

Many running backs can do all three: run, block, and catch. They might be and are, in some situations, the most valuable of all running backs because they *can* do all three. They're often described as an "every-down" back, or a complete back, meaning they will most likely stay in a game during any situation and not be replaced by a specialist.

But playing running back is not only about running the ball—not the way the game is now played, what with all the passing you'll see, there's a lot of blocking that goes with it. Routinely, a running back is held back to help protect the quarterback during a pass play, particularly if a blitz—where a linebacker or defensive back attacks the offensive backfield to sack the quarterback before he can pass the ball—is anticipated.

In the photo below, you can see the running back (21) executing a "check release" assignment. If a linebacker blitzes, he stays and blocks. If not, he releases into a pass route.

(Marc Carlson)

Of the many qualities coaches look for in a running back, most fans would think that speed would be at the top of the list. Speed is certainly up there among the top qualities coaches look for, along with durability, balance, and strength.

But the number one trait most often sought is vision—the ability to see "daylight" or openings in a defense—what is often referred to as a *crease* and burst through it. The action is so fast and furious that many running backs say they only see color, and where they don't is where they go.

Some running backs are built to deliver the big hit, and they do so with some relish and enthusiasm. Some offenses are built around the big-hit back. That's their rep.

But the simple fact is that the ability to avoid the big hit can add time to a running back's playing career which, in the NFL, averages about 3.3 years. While being able to block and catch passes will add to their playing time and the size of their paychecks.

THE ELMIRA EXPRESS

He was hated for being black and loved for his gentleness. He was admired for his athletic prowess and respected for his humility and compassion. Sportswriters called him "The Elmira Express," but he was, as one coach described him, "... a puppy dog, friendly and warm and kind."

(Elmira Star Gazette)

Even on the football field, where he was powerful and locomotive-like in blowing up opposing players who attempted to tackle him, he would, after knocking them down, run back and help them up. "We never had a kid so thoughtful and polite," his college coach said of him.

The kid in question was Ernie Davis. In a time when the struggle for civil rights dominated our daily lives, and hatred spilled into the streets and onto the football fields where Ernie played, he was the first black athlete to be chosen for college football's most coveted award.

FOOTBALL FOR MOMS AND SWEETHEARTS

Born on Dec. 14, 1939, in New Salem, PA, Davis grew up in poverty in Uniontown, a coal-mining town 50 miles south of Pittsburgh, where he was raised by caring grandparents. The honors came early and often, beginning when he started playing organized sports.

(Syracuse.com)

After his senior season in high school, more than 30 colleges and universities recruited him to join their program, but he chose to stay close to home and play for Syracuse. It was the same school at which his hero, Jim Brown, played—and who, later, was instrumental in his recruitment.

He didn't disappoint the Syracuse faithful. As a sophomore, he led the Orangemen to their only national football championship, but it was at season's end, in the Cotton Bowl against a highly-ranked Texas Longhorn team—who threw racial slurs at Davis and his two black teammates, resulting in a fight between the two teams before half-time—that Davis truly shone.

(Tip Top 25)

Texas mounted a comeback in the second half, but Syracuse prevailed, 23-14, and Davis was declared the player of the game. But it was afterward, at the banquet honoring the two teams, that Ernie's teammates shone. When told that, after receiving the MVP trophy, Ernie and his two black teammates would have to leave the dinner, the entire Syracuse team boycotted the event.

It wasn't the first time Davis was confronted with racism, and it wasn't the last. But Davis, who was a rising star on the football field during the epic rise of the civil rights movement on the streets of America, was always kind and gracious.

His gentle nature trumped hate.

(Youtube)

(Pinterest)

So it was of great significance to that movement that, in 1961 Ernie was awarded college football's most prized possession: the Heisman Trophy. The best in America. He was the first African American to be selected for that award, and he was as humble in his acceptance of it as he was in his everyday walk through life.

Later, he would be first again: the first black player to be selected "first" in the NFL draft by the Washington Redskins, then traded to his mentor's team, the Cleveland Browns.

(eBay)

The following year, he was diagnosed with leukemia. Still he managed to dress out in a Cleveland Brown

15

uniform for a preseason game with Pittsburgh in August, 1962. He was greeted by a standing ovation from the 78,000 fans in attendance. They didn't know it was also the last time he would dress out for a game. He died in his sleep on May 18, 1963. He was 23.

"I never met another human being as good as Ernie," Ben Schwartzwalder, his coach at Syracuse, said of his beloved running back.

Because the passage of time diminishes our ability to recall the past in great detail, it's easy to forget men such as Ernie when the news on TV and in the papers assaults our sensibilities with stories and images focused only on the worst about us instead of the best.

But it is that—the best—that endures, that outlives each of us. And it's why Ernie Davis and the way he lived—more than the way he died or the fact that he was black—still matters today and will continue to matter in the years to come.

RECEIVERS

(Rick Elliot)   (Mark and His Nikon)

They stretch a defense with their speed or confound it by attacking the short passing zones that border the line of scrimmage. In between the two—the deep threat and the quick threat—is the open grass in which they ply their trade and exhibit their skills. They're called receivers because they catch passes. They do so with the focus of a gymnast and the grace of an ice skater.

The primary receivers usually line up outside the formation, away from the offensive line. They're generally called wide receivers because they are—well—positioned "wide" from the formation. They have specialized skills.

The two skills most important and most prized by coaches are speed and good hands. They look for guys who can, as they say, "take the top off a defense," meaning stretch it vertically—towards the end zone—and do so quickly. If a fast receiver can't catch, he generally ends up playing defense.

Running backs also catch passes, but their primary job is to run the ball. When a running back does his job, receivers become blockers.

Another receiver who blocks during run plays but often lines up with the offensive line is the *tight end*. His position gets its name because of where he's routinely positioned on the line: at its end. It's another term for a receiver, while "tight"—as opposed to "wide"—describes how close he's positioned to the offensive line.

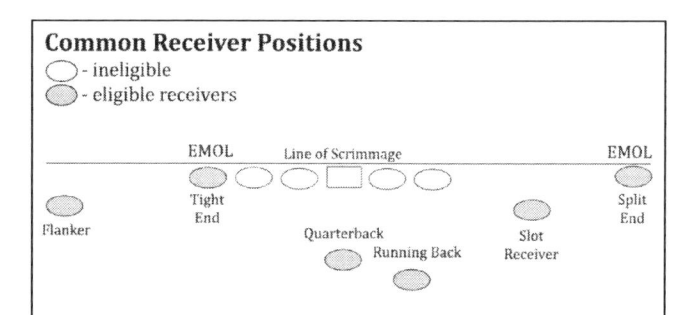

Common Receiver Positions
○ - ineligible
● - eligible receivers

EMOL   Line of Scrimmage   EMOL
Flanker   Tight End   Quarterback   Slot Receiver   Split End
Running Back

NOTE: the flanker is aligned off the line, in the backfield, so that the tight end is the *end man on the line* (EMOL) and uncovered, making him eligible. A slot receiver is positioned off the line, in the space between the offensive line and the EMOL.

Great tight ends are game changers and tough to defend because of their size and speed. They're usually bigger than wide receivers and faster than the linebackers who are often assigned to defend them. Offensive coordinators love to use tight ends to attack the middle of the field—in an area behind the middle linebacker called "the hole"—and routinely design plays that do just that. (See the slice *Tampa Two*)

Great receivers, the fast ones who can take it deep, force defenses to cover deep and not creep up close to the line of scrimmage where they can help defend against the run. Deep-threat receivers open up an offense's running attack and allow it to be balanced—an expression you'll hear TV commentators use—meaning they can throw and run as needed and not be one dimensional and easily defended.

FOOTBALL FOR MOMS AND SWEETHEARTS

In addition to the guys who are burners and take it deep, there are "possession" receivers and guys who are "quick threats." Possession receivers are the go-to-guys in situations where the offense needs yards to gain a first down or a touchdown. These guys are dependable in critical situations and rarely drop the ball.

Quick threat receivers are a quarterback's best friends because they generally operate close to the line of scrimmage. They run the short routes and get open quickly so the quarterback doesn't have to hold onto the ball too long, which allows him to avoid being tackled for a loss—what is called a "sack."

Common traits of great receivers are soft hands, an uncanny ability to find open grass, and staying focused. All of them—and I'm paraphrasing here—have a real hunger for the ball. They want the spotlight on them. The brighter, the better. They are "…precise in how they run a route and how they take it to its proper depth." They are highly competitive.

Great receivers, according to one coach, make the playbook come alive.

(Danny Wild)

SELLING THE NINE

It's football's most basic and most important pass route, and yet it's nothing more than a race to the end zone—or at least as far as the quarterback can throw.

It's called the "9" because that's the number assigned to it in most route trees—the diagram found in offensive playbooks that depicts the pass routes an offense uses. The diagram is called a tree because that's what it looks like—a tree.

Selling the 9 is a tactic. It's about deception—about convincing a defensive back that he's in that race every time a receiver releases from the line of scrimmage.

The "9" is basically a straight line. As such, it's the stem for many of the other routes a receiver can run. By "stem" we refer to another straight line, the one a receiver runs when he escapes the line of scrimmage and races to the breakpoint of his assigned route.

If a receiver can fool a defensive back into thinking he's going deep, then the underneath routes that break off the 9 open up. Separation—the goal of any receiver—becomes easier.

The deception succeeds because the 9 is a defensive back's worst nightmare. "Don't get beat deep" is the mantra he hears from his coaches. "Don't get beat deep" is what he's thinking each time a receiver lines up.

The way a receiver deceives a defensive back is by being consistent. Each time he runs a route that comes off the 9, he mimics the actions of the 9, which coaches routinely refer to as a "Go" route, or a "Take-off," or even a "Fly". Whatever it's called, it's the best trick in a receiver's bag of tricks.

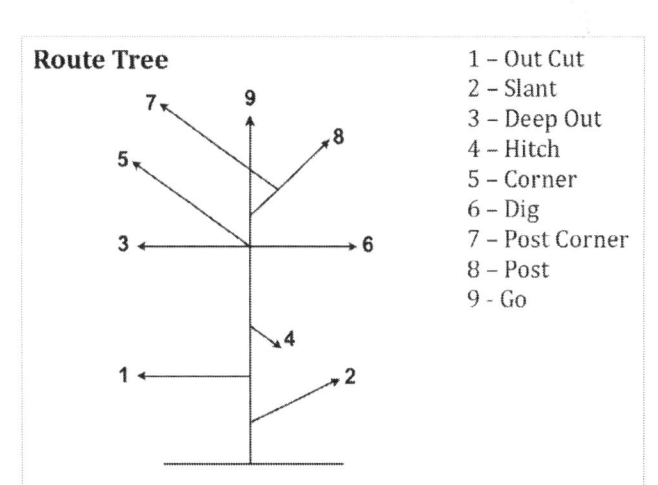

Route Tree

1 – Out Cut
2 – Slant
3 – Deep Out
4 – Hitch
5 – Corner
6 – Dig
7 – Post Corner
8 – Post
9 – Go

NOTE: this is a very simple route tree, but it illustrates why it's called a "tree." Also referred to as a "passing tree". Pass routes are routinely assigned numbers to make it easier to call plays.

THE RUN PLAY

(Brooke Novak)

The quickest way to determine what kind of play the offense is using is not to watch the backfield where the quarterback and running back(s) are positioned, but to watch the offensive line because they're not allowed to cross the line of scrimmage in a pass play, so if they do, it's a run play. The only reason they come across the line and attack the defense is to create space for the running back by moving defenders.

Run plays are bread and butter. Meat and potatoes. The good stuff. Even teams that like to throw the ball, and who do so often, have to run the ball as well, just to keep the defense guessing. But running the ball sets up the vital third part of an offense's three-pronged attack: the *play-action pass*.

Basically, there are three areas of a defense that the offense attacks with a run play: the area between the offensive tackles, called the "inside," the area over the offensive tackle, at the edge of the formation, called "off-tackle," and a defense's weakest area, which is "outside" the edge defender on the line, as shown in the graphic to below.

Areas of Attack

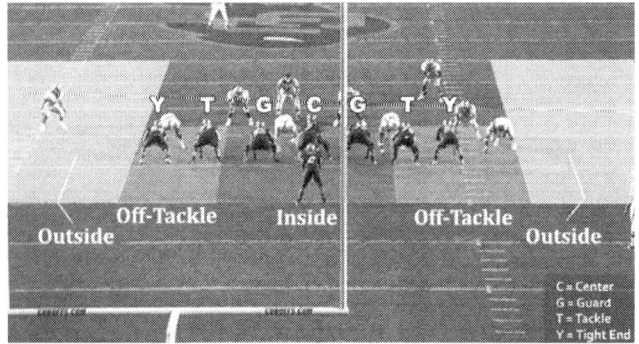

(MECU/Flickr)

How the offense attacks those areas can also be broken down into three types of run plays: those that overpower the defense, those that use speed to outflank the defense, and those that isolate a defender and "option" him. The most dangerous of the three is the option play, while the most physical is any run play attacking inside—between—the offensive tackles.

The option play creates choices—for the offense *and* the defense. Good choices for the offense, not so good for the defense. What the design of the play does is isolate a specific defender and force him to choose which of the two offensive players attacking him to defend.

If the defensive player attacks the offensive player with the ball—almost always the quarterback—the quarterback gives the ball to the running back. But if the defender attacks the running back, then the quarterback pulls the ball and runs it himself.

In either scenario the defender loses. You'll see a lot of option plays run in high school and college, especially in no-huddle, uptempo offenses. But not so much in the pros where coaches cringe at the idea of exposing their highly prized and highly paid quarterbacks to injury.

FOOTBALL'S MOST DANGEROUS PLAY

Nowadays—especially if you're watching a college game—you'll often hear TV analysts use the terms "zone read" or "read option." They're referring to offensive plays that are basically the same play—or at least the same concept—whose origin is, surprisingly, found on the hard courts of basketball; it's strategy based on the simple mathematics of the 2-on-1 fast break.

The zone read and the read option are merely variations of football's most dangerous play—the "option play"—which was first conceived by Dan Faurot back in the '40s while watching a game of round ball.

What he saw was that, in a 2-on-1 fast break, the lone defender was placed in a no-win situation. He had to make a split-second decision who to defend to prevent a score: either the ball handler or his teammate running along side, but some distance from him.

FOOTBALL FOR MOMS AND SWEETHEARTS

Spacing, Faurot noted, was critical.

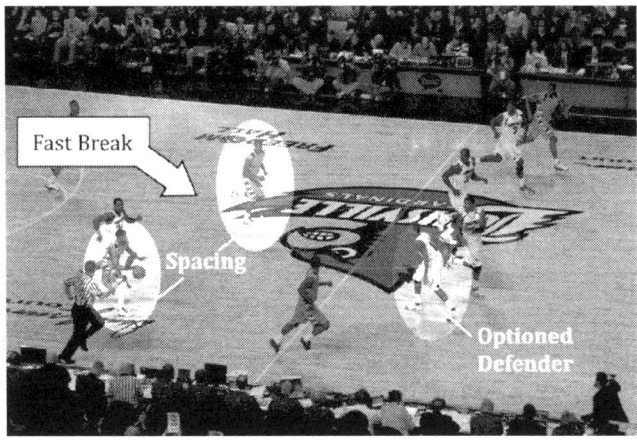

(Unknown)

If the defender chose to guard the ball handler, then the latter passed the ball to his teammate, who would drive to the goal and score. If, however, he defended the player without the ball, then the ball handler would simply drive to the goal and score. Whichever option the defender chose, he was wrong.

It's the same with the option play.

The core principle of an option play, like the fast break, is to isolate a defender and force him to choose which of the two offensive players attacking him to defend. It makes no difference what type of option is being executed or discussed, the principle is the same for all option plays. The only difference between the many types of option plays is which defender along the line of scrimmage is isolated and how.

By "isolated" we mean "unblocked." The blocking by the offensive line is schemed in such a way that the isolated defender is "read" by the quarterback. That is to say, the unblocked defender's actions are instantly analyzed by the quarterback, who either gives the ball up to another running back or keeps it himself.

An option play is being executed in the photo before. The quarterback is "reading" the unblocked defender (#7). If the defender stays, the quarterback gives the ball to the running back. If he squeezes down to tackle the running back, the quarterback keeps the ball and runs with it. This particular type of option attack is commonly called a "read option." *(Photo by Danny Wild)*

While there are several types of option plays, there are only two option concepts: the double option, which is a 2-on-1 scenario, and the triple option, which is a 3-on-2 attack. What these two methods of attack do that most traditional running plays don't is use the quarterback as a ball carrier.

In a game whose strategies are routinely based on mathematics, the defense must now account for all 11 offensive players and not simply 10. This is instrumental to the success of the option because, in all situations, the targeted defender—or defenders—must believe that the quarterback is a running threat; otherwise, there is no option, if there is no danger from him.

By threatening defenses at more than one point along the line of scrimmage, the option play forces defenses to be assignment sound and gap conscious, which routinely negates their speed, size and tactics.

It also doesn't require large and dominant offensive linemen to be successful, because the linemen don't have to sustain their blocks. They merely seal off or cut block defenders, so it is popular with teams—like the service academies—that have undersized linemen.

(Andrew Penny Photography)

And it's difficult to prepare for in a week's worth of practices, as scout teams can rarely mimic the speed and execution of a well-drilled option attack. Put simply, an option play is the best way to attack a defense, especially its perimeter where it's weakest.

19

FOOTBALL FOR MOMS AND SWEETHEARTS

While the deep pass might be football's most spectacular—if not most feared—play, defenses don't see it every play. The option is football's most dangerous play because it's almost impossible to defend, and it's a threat to go the distance any time it's run, which against an option team is every play, except when they choose to pass, which is rare.

So why don't we see the option run in the pros more often? The reasons are simple. For one, the speed and athletic ability of the pro athlete are world class. Put 11 of them on defense and the option is more easily defended than in high school and college where the abilities of the players are noticeably unequal.

The other reason—and most important—is money. Most pro coaches are reluctant to expose their multi-million dollar quarterbacks to season- or—worse—career-ending injuries, especially since great—even good—quarterbacks are few and far between.

Quarterback Getting Crushed

(Abigail Romaine)

It was once said that you might see young running quarterbacks in the pros, but you'll never see any old ones. In an option offense, quarterbacks, like the one in the picture above, get hit hard and often. One devastating hit can end a promising career and derail a money-making championship season for a pro team.

THE PASS PLAY

The pass is an air assault and is, in today's game, the most feared form of attack now that offenses are stretching defenses from sideline to sideline with exotic spread formations that create a lot of open grass.

If the offensive line can pass block for two to three seconds, offenses with middle-of-the-road talent can now compete with elite defenses because the pass which, when combined with a no-huddle, uptempo approach, is not simply an equalizer but sometimes, a defeater of defenses blessed with better talent.

The first "legal" pass was thrown on September 5, 1906, by Bradbury Robinson of St. Louis University. It was incomplete, but coaches like Knute Rockne of Notre Dame saw the advantages of it. For example, how a passing attack can force a defense to position players at the backend of the field to cover the receivers, thus weakening their defense against the run.

It's the same today. It's why defenses are structured in three levels, with the third level being defensive backs who guard potential receivers and defend against the pass. Their number, depending upon the situation, can range from three to six players. The more defenders a defense has in its backend, the fewer they have up front to stop the run.

For a pass to be legal, it must be thrown from behind the line of scrimmage. It must be thrown forward, not backward, or it is a *lateral*, which, if not caught by an offensive player, is a fumble and can be recovered by the defense. And lastly, it cannot touch the ground before being caught by an eligible receiver.

Offensive linemen are generally not eligible receivers, except in a trick play called the tackle-eligible. That's a pass play in which an offensive tackle is positioned as the last man on one side of an offensive formation and is uncovered, making him by rule an eligible receiver.

There are two kinds of pass plays. The first is a regular pass play in which the quarterback sets up in the backfield behind the offensive line and scans the defense to determine which receiver to throw to.

The second is the play-action pass in which the quarterback first executes a run fake and then sets up to throw. What the run fake does is force the defense, most particularly the linebackers, to react as if it is a run play, thus opening up space behind them which a receiver can exploit.

FOOTBALL FOR MOMS AND SWEETHEARTS

The run fake above to #21 is a precursor to the pass that will follow. You can see the linebacker outside #62 being drawn up to "plug" what he "reads" is a run play, but you can tell it's a run fake because the offensive linemen are pass blocking. They're not crossing the line of scrimmage. *(Marc Carlson)*

Play-action passes are one reason why offenses want to establish their run game. They want the defense to respect it so that, when they call a play-action pass, the defense will overreact to the run fake. The beauty of it is that, after being faked a few times, the linebackers tend to slow down, even hesitate, when they see a run play, thinking it could be a fake.

The pass play, on the other hand, especially pass plays that attack deep, stretch a defense vertically, meaning towards the end zone they are defending. This opens up the field underneath to attack from shorter pass routes.

To do that, to create the accordion effect, offenses look for fast wide receivers who can, as coaches say, "take the top off a defense." Going deep stretches a defense vertically—toward the end zone—while spread formations stretch a defense horizontally. Both create a lot of open grass for a defense to cover. That's why a defense's pass rush is so critical to stopping a pass attack (discussed under *Defending the Pass*).

When watching a no-huddle, uptempo offense, know that during his pre-snap read of the defense, the quarterback is counting the defenders "in the box"—what is technically referred to as the defensive front, the players positioned opposite the offensive line.

When their number is equal to or less than the number of players the offense has blocking, the quarterback will check off to a run play. If it's greater, the quarterback will check to a pass play because there are more players who can catch a pass than there are defenders who can prevent it.

IT WAS LEIF, NOT CHRIS

There's a three-part article on the Internet about the history of the spread offense, and nowhere in it does it mention the guy who actually created it. It's sort like what happened to Leif Erikson. You know, the guy who actually discovered America.

Historians credit Christopher Columbus with that little feat, and some of us even get a day off from work to celebrate it, but it was in fact Leif and his Vikings who arrived here 400 years before Chris, and unlike the Italian, they actually landed in North America.

(Emaze) *(The My Hero Project)*

So while it's generally agreed that Tiger Ellison introduced a version of the spread at Middletown High School in 1961, and that Jack Neumeier introduced football's first pass-based spread at Granada Hills High School back in the '70s—what he called "basketball on grass"—it was actually a guy named Rusty Russell who created the darn thing and first used it on a football field way back in the late '20s—back when spread formations went against all conventional wisdom.

Tiger — Rusty

(Pistol Triple Option Football) *(Twelve Mighty Orphans Blog)*

FOOTBALL FOR MOMS AND SWEETHEARTS

But it made perfect sense to Coach Russell, who was forced by circumstances to be innovative, if not radical. The size of the players he inherited at the Fort Worth Masonic Home dictated the need to spread defenses to create more running room.

(12 Mighty Orphans)

Not only was the school small—it averaged an enrollment of about 160 boys and girls—but so were his players. Still, despite their size, they competed against the bigger and richer "A" league schools in Texas whose enrollments numbered in the thousands.

Not one to lament a bad situation—he had been blinded by mustard gas in World War I and overcame that—Coach Russell put his players in the best possible system to succeed. And they did. A lot. Between the years 1927-1942, his "Mighty Mites"—as the orphans became known—won 127 games and lost only 30. In the 16 years he spent at the Masonic Home—a program he built from scratch—Coach Russell's teams went to the state play-offs ten times. Ten!

What he achieved was remarkable, if not simply astounding, because of the obstacles he overcame, but fundamentally, his spread system was no different than what many modern coaches like Urban Meyer at Ohio State have done since. They—like its creator—adopted the spread to run the ball. Not pass, but run.

(Twelve Mighty Orphans)

A play-off game gets the front page treatment in the Dispatch Journal in Dallas. The Model T pictured is like the one called "Old Blue" that carried the orphans to away games. The gas fumes made Coach Russell the feel drunk.

It's essentially what Dutch Meyer did at TCU in the '30s when he won over a 100 games using five receiver formations like that pictured below. He later wrote a book about it in the '50s called—are you ready for it?—Spread Formation Football.

During the '30s when the tightly-woven, power-driven Single- and Double-Wing offenses dominated football, Dutch Meyer boldly went where only Russell had gone before: he deployed his three running backs as "slot" receivers in what he called his "5 Wide" sets.

That was the term he used to describe the different formations he designed that spread and shredded defenses—what modern coaches would call an "empty set" because there's no running back in the backfield. There's only the quarterback—or what, in Dutch's day, was called the "tailback."

(Wikipedia)

The formation above looks modern, except it was in the 30's.

Meyer's spread attack produced two of college football's greatest quarterbacks in Sammy Baugh, the great thrower, and Davey O'Brien, the great runner. When Dutch saw how Baugh could, as coaches say, "spin" a football, he promptly set aside the heavy-handed double-wing attack in favor of the wide-open looks that became known as the "Meyer Spread."

The attack used many of the same principles seen in today's spread offenses. Baugh, around whom the spread was built, went on to star in the NFL, while O'Brien won the Heisman Trophy and later had an annual quarterback award named after him.

Because of the "Meyer Spread," TCU's Horned Frogs would win six Southwest Conference championships and two National championships (1935 and 1938), and Dutch Meyer, the old school coach who improved upon Rusty Russell's radical approach to offensive football, literally gave fans a peek into the game's future.

TRICKERATION

Once upon a time, a pro football team had to punt the ball on 4th down. The punter lined up about 15-yards deep, received the snap and, instead of kicking the ball, he lofted a high, tight spiral pass into the air that soared towards the return man. The return man marveled at the spin of the ball as he evaluated its trajectory while moving forward, thinking the ball was kicked high and short.

The key term here is "pass."

The offense, meanwhile, dispatched a swift receiver towards the return man. Observers of the action simply thought the receiver was a gunner intent on tackling the return man before he could advance the ball.

The receiver, however, glanced back at the ball, to gauge the path of its flight and cut in front of the return man who had positioned himself to fair catch the punt. When he did so, he struck the receiver who was knocked to the ground as the ball nosed into the turf and rolled about.

An official close to the action, withdrew his yellow flag and threw it. The return man, slightly stunned, was certain that the receiver was the offending player. But the official surprised all who were watching and called "defensive pass interference" on the return man, because what he thought was a punt, was actually a pass.

By knocking the receiver to the ground, he "interfered" with his attempt to catch the ball. What the return man thought was a punt, was actually a trick play that worked, gaining the offense a first down and a new series of downs .

Trick plays like the fake punt come in all shapes and sizes, and—hopefully—when least expected. But trick plays are, first and foremost, legal plays. There must be seven men on the line, and the players at either end of the formation cannot be covered if they are to go out for a pass. Any shift of personnel must occur before a player can go in motion, and only the players not in a 3-point stance—that is, with a hand in the ground—can change positions.

Fake punts, fake field goals, double passes, reverses and double reverses are a small sampling of the magic an imaginative offensive coordinator can and routinely does create. Every offensive coordinator has a bag of tricks. Timing—that is, when to use them—is the thing. When a trick play is used is generally determined by the flow of the game and the coach's instincts.

Sometimes, in a fourth-and-short situation, where the offense needs less than five yards for a first down, the offense will line up in an exotic formation then quickly shift and maybe shift again before sending someone in motion. The intent behind all the sudden movements is to draw a defensive lineman offsides, which would result in a five-yard penalty and a first down for the offense.

It's a trick play but not in the sense that the offense is advancing the ball by running or throwing it. The trick is to deceive a defensive lineman to react to movement, but to the movement of offensive players, not the ball—which is what he's trained to do. Sometimes though, in that particular situation, defensive linemen are so focused on penetrating and stopping the run that they react to any movement.

Tricks plays are a work of art when they work, mostly because they are unexpected and because they are so well conceived. Truly great trick plays rely on the tendencies a defense and its players have exhibited in certain situations in previous games, which offensive coaches have detected in their film studies. Often, the idea is to let the defense trick itself by using the play-action it saw on film, but not the wrinkle the offensive coaches have added that is itself the trick.

TACKLE ELIGIBLE

The tackle-eligible is an example of how coaches work the rules to their advantage. As trick plays go, it has been around awhile. But defenses are often so focused on the wide receivers in a formation that they some-

times fail to notice that, by alignment, the tackle to one side of the offensive formation is an eligible receiver. The reason he can be an eligible receiver has to do with the rules that govern all offensive formations, regardless of their arrangement

As discussed before under Formations, the end man positioned on either side of the formation and the four allowed in the backfield are eligible receivers. The offensive tackle becomes eligible when, by a formation's design, he's the end man on one side and he's "uncovered"—meaning no one is positioned outside of him, on the same line.

It's easy to miss him because the offensive tackle's jersey number is that of an offensive lineman—not a receiver—and he's positioned where an offensive tackle normally would be, which helps the deception. This is especially true versus an uptempo, no-huddle offense. They're in a hurry to line up, so defenses are too, and they sometimes don't notice the irregularity.

This Tackle Is Eligible

(SB Nation)

In this situation the offensive tackle can go past the line of scrimmage and catch a pass, but only if before the play he has informed the officials that he will be an eligible receiver. He must do that to keep from being penalized. If he doesn't, and they see an offensive lineman past the line of scrimmage in a pass play, they will penalize him for being an ineligible receiver downfield. By warning the officials beforehand, they'll know the trick play is coming and that it's legal.

The tackle eligible is a sweet little slight of hand that works great in short-yardage situations when the defense is expecting a run. And it's a great rabbit to pull out of the hat when the offense is in the red zone, looking at a short field. All too often the surprise is so complete that the offensive tackle finds himself alone in open grass, and the worry is that he'll drop the ball.

PLAY CALLING

Many factors can influence what plays an offensive coordinator calls in any given situation. The three that are perhaps the most important are *field position*, *down and distance*, and the *amount of time* left on the clock, what is commonly called clock management (discussed under *Time*).

Field position refers to where on the football field the offense must start a play. Is it close to the opponent's end zone, inside their 20-yard line—in what you'll often hear referred to as the *red zone*—or is it at midfield or even farther away? Is it worse? Is the offense lining up with their backs to their own end zone? If so, then the offensive coordinator might choose to run safe plays that don't risk a turnover or the ballcarrier being tackled in the end zone for a *safety*.

But if you watch football on TV, "down and distance" is an expression you'll hear used quite often. It's the single most important aspect of a game because of how it influences the strategies and tactics that coaches use, both on offense and defense. And it's probably the one aspect of the game least understood by football fans.

A "down" is often described as a "play," but actually, it's an opportunity to run a play, which is nothing more than an attempt to advance the ball towards an opponent's end zone. A play starts with the snap of the ball and ends when the ballcarrier is tackled or falls to the ground (except in pro football where the ballcarrier has to be touched by an opponent to be downed).

Only offenses run plays; defenses react to them.

> **Where did "downs" come from—**
>
> *Like the game itself, our system of downs—or at least the term—got its start in rugby. The player carrying the ball would declare himself "held!" when he was tackled and couldn't advance the ball. At that point, his tacklers would say, "Have it down," and the ballcarrier would put the ball down.*
>
> *To reduce the practice of "sandbagging"—in which teams purposely played slow—Walter Camp—the*

FOOTBALL FOR MOMS AND SWEETHEARTS

father of American football—introduced the first systems of "downs" in 1880 which gave the offense three plays to gain five yards or give up the ball.

A game in 1902

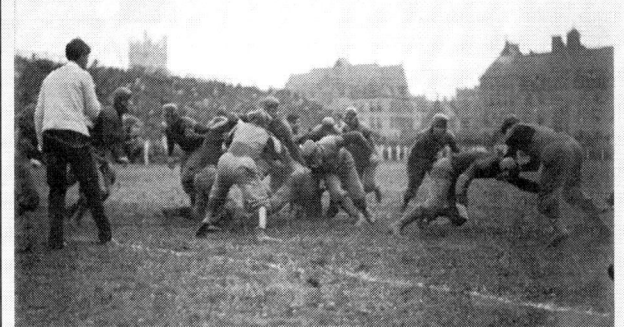

(Tip Top 25)

Then, after the forward pass was adopted in 1906, offenses were given four downs to gain 10 or more yards or give up the ball. A procedure that's still in use today.

What adds to the suspense of a game is that offenses have only four downs to gain the yardage needed to be awarded another series of four downs. What is called a "first down." If they don't, they must punt the ball to the opposing team, and they rou-tinely do so on fourth down.

So in actuality, the offense only has three downs, or three opportunities, to earn a first down or score. What plays the offensive coordinator chooses to use, given the distance the offense must travel to gain a first down, are often determined before the game is played.

Play calling might look like guesswork, but by studying game film of his opponent's defense, a coach can analyze their personnel—their individual weaknesses and strengths—and the defense's tendencies, that is, what tactics and schemes they favor during a particular down-and-distance situation. It's called game planning. What Sun Tzu, the Chinese general who wrote the book on how to fight a war, referred to as "... knowing your enemy."

Often, you'll see a coach on the sideline referring to a massive, color-coded chart. The chart, assembled in the days prior to the game, categorizes all the probable down-and-distance situations, like first and long, or third and short, or second and medium, with the number being the "down" and the descript-

tor referring to the "distance" needed for a first down. Under each situation is a list of plays that can be called in anticipation of the tactics and schemes the defense will most likely use in that situation.

Flop Chart

(John Martinez Paviglia)

While it's for sure coaches often go with their gut, what their experience has taught them, especially when they make adjustments to their game plan based on what the defense is doing, they most often go with what they know about their opponent, what their opponent has done in previous games and are likely to do again in a certain down-and-distance situation.

It's not rocket science, but neither is it guesswork.

THE NEW MATH

Play calling isn't simply about down-and-distance or an opponent's tendencies, though both factor into an offensive coordinator's thinking, but often it's about numbers. That is, the number of defenders the defense has in the "box."

If you watch games on TV, especially college games, you'll often see an uptempo, no-huddle offense line up as if it's going to initiate a play, when suddenly, all of the skill players straighten up and look to the sideline like they're a bunch of meerkats who spotted some food.

What's happening is that the offensive coordinator has had a chance to see what scheme the defense is using, and either he or an assistant is signaling in the play call from the sideline.

Chances are, too, that he has counted the number of defenders in the "box" and has decided to run the ball if their number is five, or pass if their number is great-

25

er. A quarterback does the same thing during his pre-snap read and, in most cases, has the authority to check out of a bad play and into a good one based n the numbers.

Above: the defense in the photo above is in the dark uniforms, facing you. What you're looking at is normally called the defensive front, but in coachspeak, it's called "the box." It usually consists of the defensive line and the linebackers. When the quarterback begins his pre-snap read, he can see seven, maybe eight defenders in the box which makes it strong versus the run and weak versus the pass. *(LOC Photography)* Below: there's six in the box but there's six to block them, so this would be a good time to run the ball. *(LOC Photography)*

You run against five because the offense has five offensive linemen who can block them. But you pass if it's greater because, conversely, there will be fewer defenders in the secondary to protect against the pass.

Often in this situation the running back is kept in the backfield to help pass block for the quarterback because if there are six or more in the box, there's a strong likelihood that the defense is planning to blitz.

Using the same math, quarterbacks are often given the greenlight to "check out" of a "bad" play and into a "good" one because of the scheme the defense is using. Checking out of a bad play and into a good one is a game within a game: a game of numbers.

IDENTIFYING OFFENSES

Offenses can often be identified by their formations and their function, what they force a defense to do to counter their arrangement of players. There are basically four kinds of offenses. The *spread*—which you'll see a lot of. The *heavy* in which the offense is compact and looking like a bulldozer. The *pro-style*, which is most often the "I" formation. And the *option* offense, whose base formation is routinely balanced.

Spread offenses rely on a variety of formations that "spread" or stretch a defense from sideline to sideline. Most often you'll see three receivers on one side and one on the other. In coach speak, there's a generic reference to them as 3x1 or 1x3 formations), or 2x2—meaning two to the left and two to the right.

The 3x1 (or 1x3) formations take advantage of the wide and shortside of the field created when the ball is spotted at a hashmark (see *The Field and its Features*). The 2x2 look is most often used when the ball is spotted near the middle of the field between the hashmarks.

Example of a 3x1 (or 1x3) Formation

Read from the left to the right. Flip it, and you have a 1x3.

(Smart Football)

Example of a 2x2 Formation

(The Football Brainiacs)

The idea behind a spread look is to create space and force the defense to choose between defending against the pass or the run. Defending against the pass means putting more players in the secondary than in the box to defend against the run, and vice versa.

Heavy formations—what some coaches call jumbo formations—pack it in. They bring in the big bodies, tighten the *line splits*, and look to pound the rock—meaning overpower the defense and run the ball. Play-action pass plays from this look are very effecttive because the defense is often anticipating a run play, and for this reason heavy formations are often used in short-yardage situations, where the offense only needs a few yards to get a first down or to score.

Pro-style or conventional formations combine the effects of both spread and heavy formations. The most popular is the "I" formation. It can run with power because it routinely has an extra blocker—a tight end—on one side of the formation and two running backs lined up directly behind the quarterback. The one up front—the fullback—routinely serves as a lead blocker for the primary running back positioned behind him, who is often called the "I-back" or "tailback."

The "I" can also spread a defense, at least the cornerbacks, because it has a wide receiver positioned on either side of the formation. The wide receiver to the tight end's side is lined up in the backfield, though, so that he doesn't cover the tight end, which makes him an eligible receiver as well and, as such, a threat to catch a pass.

So by formation alone the "I" can release three or four receivers into pass routes or run with power because of the fullback lead blocking at the point of attack. But the killer thing the "I" can do better than many offensive systems is play-action passes because of the constant threat of the run. (For an explanation of the play-action pass, refer to *The Pass Play* section.)

Option offenses are seen in the college and high school game and not in the pros. Pro coaches might use an option play in their scheme, but generally, they don't want to use an offense that has their quarterback running more than throwing. The risk of injury is too great, and they have big-time running backs who are paid big money to do exactly that.

The most famous option offense was the *Wishbone*, but anymore, that has been replaced by the *Flexbone*, whose base formation is balanced, meaning there are an equal number of players on either side of the center and their alignments are mirrored..

By presenting a balanced look, the offense forces the defense to do the same, which makes attacking it easier, particularly because the blocking up front is simplified. But because the option attack is an equalizer and difficult to prepare for in one week, it allows small schools with smaller athletes to compete with, and often beat, bigger schools fielding bigger players.

(Henry deSaussure Copeland)

In the previous photo, the defense on the left is mirroring the arrangement of players in the offense on the right. The offensive arrangement is balanced because there is an equal number of players on either side of the center.

Despite all the passing you'll see, and the variety of formations, the option play is still football's most dangerous run play, and it is why you'll see it used in some form in *all* offenses.

LONESOME POLECAT

Chances are that if you see the Lonesome Polecat, you'll wonder what the hell is that? Defenses did as well back in 1958 when they first saw the formation displayed on a football field.

The odd configuration of players was born of desperation when Middletown High School (OH) was looking at its first losing season ever. After several sleepless nights spent conjuring up different schemes that fit the skills of his players, Glenn Ellison—affectionately called "Tiger" because of his eloquent and motivating half-time speeches—finally tossed aside the heavy-handed offense he was using in favor of a wide-open attack that looked like something drawn in the dirt of a playground.

FOOTBALL FOR MOMS AND SWEETHEARTS

And in a way it was.

While driving to work one morning, Tiger observed kids playing at a school playground. While watching them, he realized—and correctly it would seem—that that is where kids first learn to play football: on a playground.

The offense he fashioned from that morning's epiphany was strange, but the results weren't. The team won its last five games to finish the campaign 5-4-1, and Glenn Ellison's unique attack was permanently installed in football lore as the Lonesome Polecat.

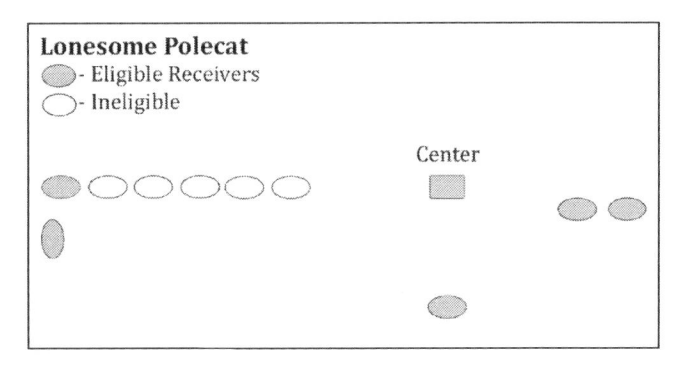

Lonesome Polecat
- Eligible Receivers
- Ineligible
- Center

But Tiger didn't rest on his laurels. In the off season, he tinkered with his creation like a teenage boy souping up his first car, and he opened the following season with an offensive system that would, in the hands and mind of a guy named Mouse Davis, shatter records and appear in four Super Bowl losses as the offense of choice for the Buffalo Bills.

Tiger christened the offense the Run-'n-Shoot because the quarterback ran around in the backfield, looking for an open receiver, and when he saw one he'd "shoot" him the ball. It was very much like what the quarterbacks do on playgrounds and what they did in the Lonesome Polecat. But its descendant was better organized and actually had several coordinated pass plays.

In Tiger's new and expunded offense, the receivers ran what are called "option routes." A receiver could—and would—change his pass route based on what the defense was doing to cover them. What's called a "sight adjustment." The quarterback, meanwhile, would "read" them, knowing what options they had to choose from.

It was truly ingenious, and a real pain in the butt to defend.

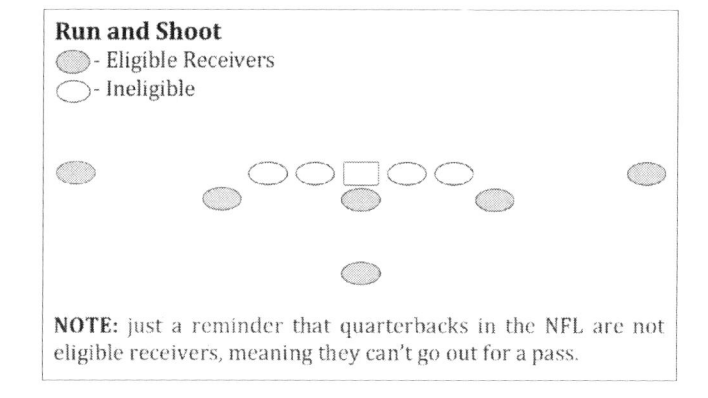

Run and Shoot
- Eligible Receivers
- Ineligible

NOTE: just a reminder that quarterbacks in the NFL are not eligible receivers, meaning they can't go out for a pass.

It became even more painful when, facing a similar situation as the head coach of Portland State, Mouse Davis adopted the offense because of his "pissants."

(Oregon Local News)

These were the small players Davis inherited when he took over the program in 1974. Davis, only 5'5" and 135 lbs, was himself diminutive in size when he played college ball. Hence, the moniker "Mouse."

Davis had won a state championship as a high school coach using the Run-'n-Shoot. He realized that his "pissants" couldn't compete with other college programs using a run-based offense, so he went to the Run-'n-Shoot because it maximized his players skills. With Neil Lomax and June Jones operating as quarterbacks, Portland State rewrote the offensive record book for the NCAA, setting all-time highs in yards gained passing the ball.

Neil | June

(Sports Training)    (The Voice of Kapolei)

The offense reached the pinnacle of the mountain when, using a much improved version of Tiger's creation, the Buffalo Bills played in four straight Super Bowls and lost each one, but recorded pro football's greatest 2nd half comeback in a play-off game.

The strange offense—which looks a lot like the Swinging Gate formation discussed under the Special Teams section—confused defenses at first. But even more so when it grew up and became the Run-'n-Shoot.

But, as with many offensive innovations that sprang up and destabilized the balance of power between offenses and defenses, the defense caught up with it and the offense faded from general use. But many of its principles are still in use in the spread attacks now populating the football landscape, even though the Run-'n-Shoot itself has come to occupy a unique place in football history.

Just like its parent, the Lonesome Polecat.

DEFENSE

The defense is the team opposing the offense's efforts to score. It does that by tackling the ballcarrier and thwarting the offense's attempts to gain a first down. When it does that, the offense has to surrender possession of the ball by punting it to the defense.

Regardless of the level of competition, defenses are structured in three levels: the defensive line, the linebackers, and the defensive backs. The players assigned to each level have specific responsibilities based on their roles in the scheme, and their positions are given specific names, the most common of which are identified in the graphic below.

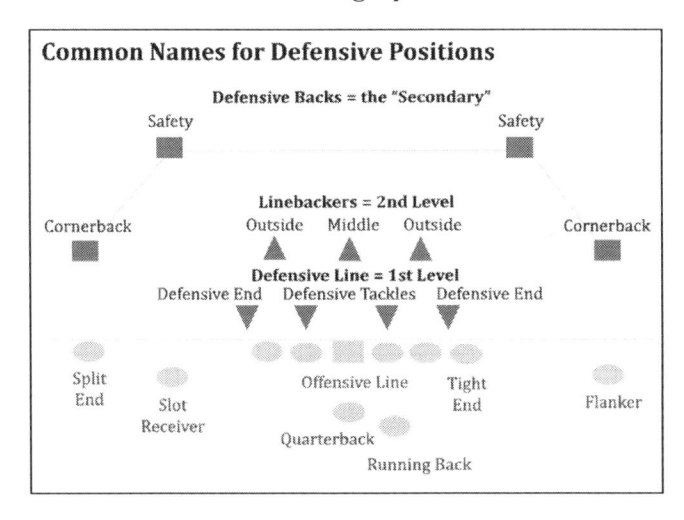

Common Names for Defensive Positions

Defensive Backs = the "Secondary"
Safety   Safety
Cornerback   Linebackers = 2nd Level   Cornerback
Outside Middle Outside
Defensive Line = 1st Level
Defensive End Defensive Tackles Defensive End

Split End   Slot Receiver   Offensive Line   Tight End   Flanker
Quarterback
Running Back

But defenses, especially in the NFL, rarely look like they're on three levels. Defensive players will routinely line up in fake positions before the ball is snapped to disguise the scheme the defense will use after.

The idea is to confuse offenses who, during the "pre-snap read" of the defense, are trying to decipher the defense's intent by the position of its players.

So how can you tell who's who in a defense? Look at the "Box," at the players positioned opposite the offensive line. The players inside the Box are most often the defensive line and the linebackers. The players outside the Box—those lined up opposite a wide receiver and deep, at the backend of the defense—are most often the defensive backs.

THE OKIE

It's called the Okie because it was developed at the University of Oklahoma. The 5-2 alignment—five defensive linemen and two linebackers—became football's dominant defense back in the 50's. It is still used at the high school and youth levels, and can be seen today in the NFL and college game as its offspring: the 3-4.

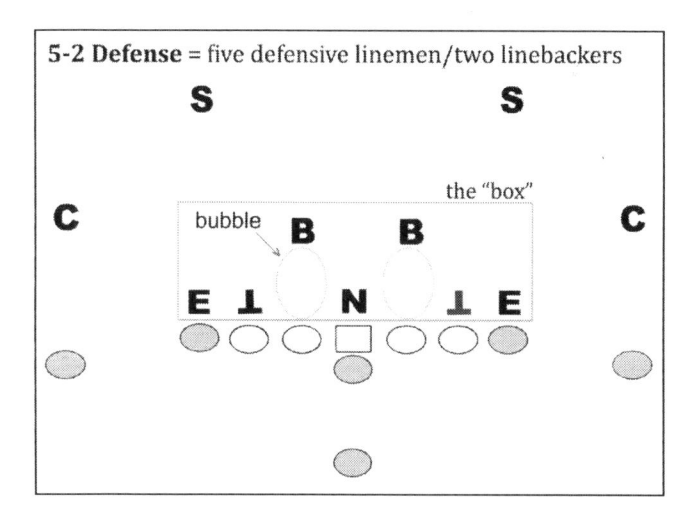

5-2 Defense = five defensive linemen/two linebackers

S   S

the "box"
C   bubble B   B   C
E T   N   T E

It's creator, a guy who strung together a record 47 wins in a row, explained that he dusted off the run-stuffing 7-2 defense—used back in the '30s—and modified it to defeat the option attack known as the Split-T and other run-based offenses he confronted in the '50s.

That defense, the 7-2, permitted its defensive ends—

the last guy on either side of the defensive line—to drop off into pass coverage. So did Bud Wilkinson's "Okie." Not only that, it also allowed the inside linebackers, who are aligned in the "bubble" opposite the offensive guards, to quickly decipher the play based on how the guards blocked.

The Okie is still used by many high school and youth football teams because it's easy to learn and allows coaches to focus on teaching technique. But because of the increased use of the pass, college and pro coaches needed more speed and better skills to defend it, so they replaced the defensive ends in the Okie with outside linebackers, and the 5-2 became the 3-4. Same look but improved speed and skills.

It's weakness is that, because it's a 2-gap scheme, the 3-4 needs specialized talent on the defensive line. The nose tackle—the guy opposite the center—and the two defensive ends, who are now positioned inside—opposite the offensive tackles—have to be big, bad, and powerful, which is explained in the slice under the Defending the Run section. It's strength, though, is in blitzing. It can attack in a variety of ways.

DEFENSIVE LINE

(Dan Schuleman)

The first line of defense in any scheme is the defensive linemen. They are the players aligned closest to the ball and opposite the offensive line. They are easily recognized as they are most often in a 3-point stance. But depending upon the scheme being used, some defensive linemen can be upright, in a 2-point stance.

A defensive line is comprised of defensive tackles and defensive ends. The defensive tackles are positioned between the defensive ends who are, as their name implies, at the end of the line, either on or outside the end man on the offensive line.

The first job of the defensive line is to shut down the run. They do that by controlling the "gaps" between offensive linemen; that is, the space between them. It's a strategy called "gap control." Each defensive lineman and linebacker is assigned a gap to defend. The defensive linemen take on the offensive linemen, defeat their blocks, and if the ballcarrier attacks their assigned gap, they tackle him. And if he attacks elsewhere, they pursue him.

In the photo above, the defensive linemen (in white uniforms), have shed their blocks and are preparing to attack—"rush"—the quarterback through their assigned gap in the offensive line. *(Photo by Darrell Marquette)*

Seems simple enough, but it isn't. Playing defensive line not only takes great strength and quickness off the ball—which translates into a player's speed at the snap of the ball, his explosiveness—but great instincts as well. Defensive linemen routinely recognize what kind of attack the offense is using, be it a run play or a pass, based on the blocking of the offensive line.

Are the offensive linemen firing across the line and attempting to move the defensive line to make space for a running back, or are they retreating to set up a protective wall behind which the quarterback can "read" the defense and throw? One is a run play, the other a pass, but in each scenario a defensive linemen doesn't want to stay blocked. He needs to be free to pursue the ballcarrier or rush the quarterback.

The job of the defensive end is a little more complicated than that of the defensive tackle because of his position on the line. As the end man on the line, he most often has "contain" responsibility, meaning his job is to make sure the ballcarrier doesn't get outside of him and into the perimeter where the defense is weakest. In coachspeak, this is called "setting the edge," with the edge being the end of the offensive line.

In the photo above, #90—a defensive end—is setting the edge. By position alone, he's forcing the ballcarrier (#24) back inside where he can be tackled by #50—the linebacker preparing to "plug" the hole in the offensive line. (Photo by Guy Herbert)

This is a critical job because defenses know that offenses want to attack where they are weakest. It's called the "outside" because it's literally outside the offensive line, and it's the weakest area in a defense because it has a lot of open grass, and only a few players to defend it.

Being the player responsible for outside containment is the toughest job. It's very stressful because a lot can go wrong, and when it does, everybody sees it. When the contain defender—the guy generally at the edge of a formation—sees a hard fake inside, his first instinct is to attack it and stop what he thinks is an inside run play. "Staying home"—which is coachspeak for holding his ground—and forcing the play back inside if it bounces out takes discipline.

In offensive plays seeking to attack outside, the contain defender is the focal point of the attack. Offenses will either "read" him or block him. When they choose to read him—when they "option" him—they leave him unblocked and force him to choose: either crash inside or stay home. The quarterback will read his reaction and counter it.

But when they choose to block him, it's either with a lead blocker—a running back, most likely a fullback—or an offensive lineman pulling from the opposite side of the formation. Defeating the option takes discipline. Defeating the block takes strength.

Often, you'll see defensive linemen execute a "stunt"—especially during a pass play—in which they switch assignments and charge different gaps in an attempt to confuse the offensive line. Even then they are assigned a specific gap to defend, and the defensive lineman charging at the end of the line will have "contain" responsibility.

Containing and pursuing the ballcarrier—be it a run-ning back attempting to escape the backfield and penetrate the defense or the quarterback setting up to throw the ball—is the principal responsibility of the defensive linemen. The better they do their jobs the less a defense has to use a linebacker or defensive back to attack the offensive backfield, and the more of a surprise it is when they do.

That's called *blitzing*.

TECHNIQUES

If you watch a lot of football on TV, you'll often hear the color analyst refer to a defensive lineman as a "3-technique," or maybe a "5," or even a "zero." What he's describing is where along the line the defensive lineman is positioned opposite the offensive line.

Years ago, as far back as the '50s, a high school coach in Texas started using numbers to identify defensive linemen positions. His name was Bum Phillips. He later became a famous pro coach with the Houston Oilers.

Bum was the winningest coach in franchise history. He never wore his hat in a domed stadium because, as he explained it, his mom taught him better. (Photo by YouTube)

Bum not only numbered the different positions but assigned to each position specific "techniques" the

FOOTBALL FOR MOMS AND SWEETHEARTS

defensive lineman should use to defeat the offensive lineman opposite him and defend his space on the line.

Each position had a specific stance, specific footwork, and specific responsibilities based on the lineman's proximity to the ball or the edge of the offensive line. In time, those numbered positions became known as "techniques" and the linemen by the number assigned to the technique they played.

In the "technique" system a defensive lineman can be positioned "head-up" on the offensive lineman or on a shoulder—what coaches call a "shade."

(John Martinez Paviglia)

The positions are numbered 0-9, with "0" being head-up on the center. The even numbers represent the helmet-on-helmet or "head-up" alignments, while the odd numbers represent the "shade" alignments in which the defensive lineman is partially positioned in a gap and threatening it.

Where the system can be confusing to a fan is at the edge of an offensive formation where the numbers 7, 8, and 9 are flipped around to maintain the "even" and "odd" number system.

Another hiccup is the inside shade alignments on the offensive guards and tackles because there are more alignments than single-digit numbers, so "2i" and "4i" are assigned to them. They translate into "2 inside" and "4 inside."

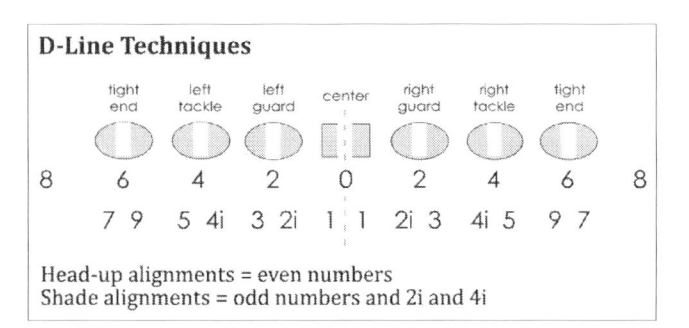

D-Line Techniques

tight end	left tackle	left guard	center	right guard	right tackle	tight end
8	6	4	2	0	2	4	6	8
	7 9	5 4i	3 2i	1	1	2i 3	4i 5	9 7

Head-up alignments = even numbers
Shade alignments = odd numbers and 2i and 4i

It used to be that everybody lined up the same way. A defensive lineman would align opposite an offensive lineman, and for four quarters they'd battle each other, mano a mano.

But as offenses became more sophisticated, defenses followed, and the responsibilities of the defensive lineman changed based on where he played on the line. By assigning a "technique" to a specific alignment, a defensive line coach can make quick and specific adjustments to combat the schemes the offense is using.

LINEBACKER

(Robert Welch)

Linebackers are the studs on defense. If anyone is missing any teeth, it's probably them. They occupy a very strategic position in a defense: they are, as their name implies, in "back" of the "line." They're the defense's second level, the guys operating in that space between the defensive line and the defensive backs who form the secondary.

Guys who play linebacker have a very unique skill set in that they're asked to plug holes at the line and stop the run, so they have to be strong and balls-to-the-wall. But they also need lateral speed to chase down a ballcarrier running toward the sideline. That's just to stop the run.

Against the pass, they routinely drop into coverage and defend a zone or a specific receiver, so they have to have good hips to change direction. And they're often called upon to blitz the quarterback and sack him before he can throw the ball.

Against the run, they must have the strength to take on blocks and "plug" holes that appear in the offensive line as the blocking develops. They need speed to pursue plays from sideline to sideline.

FOOTBALL FOR MOMS AND SWEETHEARTS

The multiple assignments require multiple skills. The most important is perhaps their ability to read. Not words, but their *keys*—a specific thing the offense is doing that telegraphs what the play is and where the ball is going—so they can react to it quickly and accurately.

The most important linebacker is the "Mike," which is coachspeak for the middle linebacker. He's generally a badass and the leader of the defense, the one who receives the "calls" from the sideline as to what scheme to use and, if the defense huddles, shares it with the others. But anymore, the game is so fast that defenses rarely if ever huddle, and everyone looks to the sideline for the defensive signals.

He's the best athlete of the linebackers, the one who can cover ground from sideline to sideline to tackle a ballcarrier, and the one who can take on a block and plug a hole. He can also cover the middle of the field—that area beneath the deep middle where the safeties operate—against the pass. And now that mobile quarterbacks are becoming the "in" thing on offense, he needs to have the speed to "spy" the quarterback wherever he goes and tackle him if he decides to run.

Because he's in the middle of all the action, and because he's probably the baddest dude of the 11 on defense, he's the captain. The one who makes all the calls and changes to the scheme based on what the offense is doing.

Something you'll see quite often in a game is the quarterback pointing to the "Mike" linebacker as he settles in behind the center. What he's doing is telling the offensive line where the Mike is so they can adjust their blocking scheme to his location in the defensive front—what is usually called "the box." (Photo by Rick Elliot)

Two other terms TV commentators use when identifying linebackers are the "Sam" and the "Will." Like Mike, they're coachspeak. They refer to two linebacker positions. The first one—the Sam—is generally positioned to the "strongside" of an offensive formation. That's the side with the most blockers, generally a tight end. He is routinely lined up next to an offensive tackle who can catch passes but, because he's also an extra blocker, makes his side of the formation stronger than the other.

The Sam is a stud. A very strong and physical player who can "set the edge" if called upon. That is, take on a lead blocker and prevent a ballcarrier from escaping the backfield and getting outside where the defense is weakest. He also covers the tight end if he releases beyond the line of scrimmage to run a pass route.

But football has changed a lot since the Sam position was first associated with the strongside. Offenses have changed. And so has the Sam's role in a defense. He's more versatile. Capable of taking on blocks, as well as dropping into coverage and, when his number is called, blitzing.

The same can be said of the Will, who is routinely aligned on the weakside—the side of an offensive formation with the fewest blockers. He's generally the fastest of the linebackers, but again, offenses—the way they stretch a defense to throw the ball as well as run a lot of option plays using the quarterback as a running back—have forced defensive coaches to select a Will who can operate in space as well as close to the line of scrimmage. The Will is a blend of the best in a safety and that in a linebacker.

33

FOOTBALL FOR MOMS AND SWEETHEARTS

(Robert Welch)

Where you'll see the three linebackers most often is with teams that favor the 4-3 defense: four defensive linemen and three linebackers. They're also present in the other popular defense, the 3-4. The fourth linebacker in the 3-4 scheme is often called the Jack. He's sort of like the Will. Very versatile. Very strong. And very fleet-footed. He's both a run-stuffer and a pass defender.

You'll often hear linebackers referred to by a variety of names. The standard acronyms, however, and those most understood and used by coaches, players and TV commentators, are those described above: the Mike, the Sam, the Will, and, if there are four, the Jack. Maybe he's called the Jack because, like most linebackers, he does it all and is, by virtue of his job description, a "jack" of all trades.

While linebackers are often used to defend against the pass, especially now with the increased use of the pass and spread offenses, their primary job is to stop the run.

FOOTBALL'S TOUGHEST TACKLE

It was Germany Schulz who many claim invented the linebacker position at the University of Michigan in 1904 by simply standing up when he played defense. He was also the center on offense, which was not unusual back in the day.

Prior to 1941, football players routinely played both ways—meaning on defense and offense. It was called "iron-man football." Then, when the big war came, teams had problems finding and fielding highly-skilled players because almost all were in uniform and fighting a war, so unlimited substitutions were allowed.

(Youtube)

But in 1953, because of money, football went back to using two-way players until 1964, when separate platoons for defense and offense were established. And that's how it is now. We have separate platoons of specialized players for the offense and defense and, in some cases, even special teams.

The last of the "Sixty-Minute Men" was a big-hitting war veteran who, like Schultz, played linebacker and center and in the off season sold concrete. His name was Charles Phillip Bednarik. He was the son of Slovakian immigrants and played his college ball at the University of Pennsylvania, where he was a three-time All American.

This was after he had flown 30 combat missions as a waist gunner on a B-24. The anti-aircraft fire was so thick, he recalled, "you could walk on it." Then in 1949, he was the first player selected in the pro draft by the Philadelphia Eagles, for whom he played both center and middle linebacker until he retired.

Chuck Bednarik = at Penn, a 3-time All-American.

(YouTube)

34

FOOTBALL FOR MOMS AND SWEETHEARTS

B-24 Bomber over Nazi Germany.

Nicknamed "Concrete Charlie" because of his toughness and durability—he missed only three games in 14 seasons with the Eagles.

He's not only famous for having been pro football's last true two-way player but also for the devastating tackle he delivered on New York Giants running back Frank Gifford in a game on November 20, 1960. The tackle was—reportedly—so hard that Gifford was knocked unconscious and didn't play football again until 1962.

Over a year later.

(Slate)

Sportswriters of the time described the tackle as a deliberate attempt to injure Gifford. Even now, Yahoo declares that it was "... one of the hardest hits the game has ever seen." That Bednarik appeared to celebrate the tackle while Gifford lay unconscious on the ground only added to the general opinion that Concrete Charlie—the toughest man in pro football at the time—sought to harm Gifford.

A replay of the tackle, however, as grainy as it is, clearly shows that Gifford tried to avoid Bednarik, that Bednarik reached back with his arm and the two collided—shoulder to shoulder—and that, because of the collision, Gifford went to the ground hard. What Gifford revealed later is that he wasn't knocked unconscious when Bednarik hit him but when his head struck the frozen turf.

In the absence of instant replay, sportswriters—seemingly bent on amplifying the hit in the minds of their readers—exaggerated the facts. They described the tackle as "violent" and "vicious," and even went so far as to accuse Bednarik of targeting Gifford.

But it was the picture of Concrete Charlie standing over the fallen Gifford and pumping his fist that inflamed most people. Not with outrage or disgust, as might be expected, but with an excitement and glee that—fueled by the faulty news reports—rose to the level of a gladiatorial spectacle.

Asked later about the tackle and apparent taunting, Bednarik explained that pumping his fist was an end of the game victory signal that he performed routinely, and if people thought he was "gloating over Frank, [then] they're full of you know what."

The last of the "Sixty-Minute Men" passed away on March 21, 2015, at the age of 89. He was voted an All Pro eight times, selected as one of the best 100 players to ever play the game, and was enshrined in pro football's Hall of Fame one year after retiring. But that for which he's best remembered could—in the parlance of our time—easily qualify as "fake news."

DEFENSIVE BACK

Defensive backs form the third line of defense, even though as a unit they're routinely referred to as the *secondary*. Generally, they're a four-man unit comprised of two cornerbacks, who cover an offense's widest and generally fastest receivers, and two safeties whom you'll often see deployed deep in the middle of the field. Their primary responsibility is to defend against the pass, but they're very active in run support and are sometimes seen blitzing the offensive backfield.

Anymore though, with the rise of uptempo, no-huddle offenses that routinely send four to five receivers past the line of scrimmage to catch passes, the third line of defense has become the most important line of defense. Frequently, it is augmented by a fifth defensive back, called the *nickel back*, and sometimes a sixth, called a *dime back*.

The "Nickel" Back

(247 Sports)

The thing to remember is that when a defense inserts extra defensive backs, it has to pull personnel from the defensive front—like a lineman or a linebacker. So when it strengthens its pass defense, it weakens its run defense. (See *The New Math* under the *Play Calling* section.)

Defensive backs, particularly the cornerbacks who often play "on an island"—meaning they're by themselves and have no help from the deep safeties—are fast and can change direction quickly because of the speed and shiftiness of the receivers they must cover.

Safeties are like hybrid linebackers though. They have some size and strength because they come up from their positions deep in the defensive backfield and help stop running plays.

They also have to cover a lot of ground when defending against the pass because of their routine positions in the deep halves of the field. And they must know how to "read"—analyze—the offensive play and react properly because they are, literally, the last line of defense.

ONE- AND TWO-HIGH SAFETIES

One aspect of a defense that can help you understand what they're doing is to look at the defensive backs routinely positioned at the defense's back end. In each case, be it one or two, their number is a clue to the defense's intent, which is why quarterbacks generally start their pre-snap "read' of a defense by analyzing the guys positioned in the deep middle of the field.

Those guys are the safeties. There's a free safety and a strong safety. Because they're so far off the ball—usually about 15-20 yards from the line of scrimmage—they're the last line of defense and in the best position to give help to the defensive backs aligned underneath them should a receiver go deep. If there's one safety back there, the look is referred to as "1-high safety" or a "single-high safety." If two, though, then it's considered a "2-high safety" scheme.

When there's one safety positioned in the deep middle of the field, it generally means the defense is going to be aggressive and blitz. If two, then they're playing it a little safer and protecting against a deep pass.

In a 1-high safety scheme, the lone defender in the back end is the free safety. The strong safety has been moved closer to the line of scrimmage—or "dropped down"—either to help defend against the run, blitz, or cover a receiver man to man. Generally, the coverage underneath a 1-high safety is man to man, while the free safety is playing zone on top, meaning he helps cover any receiver who enters the deep end of the field.

That's a lot of work because it's a lot of ground to cover, particularly if the offense sends more than one receiver deep, which is a weakness in this scheme. So, as you might expect, the free safety has to be fast. And smart.

In a 2-high safety scheme, both the free safety and the strong safety are positioned at the backend of the defense. The field back there is divided into "halves," and each safety is responsible for his half. This defense offers more protection against a deep pass, but it's

FOOTBALL FOR MOMS AND SWEETHEARTS

weaker against the run, especially if the coverage underneath the safeties is man to man, because the defenders are watching their assigned receiver and not the quarterback, which they'd be doing were they in zone coverage.

Each arrangement has its strengths and weaknesses, so defensive coordinators rely on the field situation and the flow of the game—their gut instincts—to decide when to use one or the other scheme. Just remember that what you see before the ball is snapped can rapidly change afterward, and suddenly, the offense is looking at three or four defensive backs in the deep end of the field. Game-time strategy—that is, the battle of wits between opposing coaches—has often been compared to a game of chess. It's not. It's much faster.

DEFENDING THE RUN

(Emporia State University)

Not unlike the offensive team, the speed and athletic abilities of the defensive players will determine the kinds of schemes a defense will use. As the level of competition increases from youth football to the pros, so will the variety and complexity of the schemes a defense can—and will—use because the players are simply better at each level.

Defeating a run play involves very specific responsibilities. It's a coordinated attack. It's not simply about chasing the guy with the ball and tackling him, though at times it may appear as such.

When a ballcarrier is prevented from breaking free of the defense and scoring, *force, spill and pursuit* are at work. You can think of them as jobs because, basically, that's what they are. Certain defenders, based on where they're positioned in a particular defensive scheme, are assigned one of these jobs.

Let's start with job one: "force." In simple terms, the player assigned force or "contain" responsibility literally—or more accurately, physically—turns the ballcarrier back into the "pursuit" coming from the "spill" players. The force player's job is to "set the edge." That is, he prevents the ballcarrier from getting outside where the defense is weakest.

The "spill" players, meanwhile, are the guys in the defensive front. They shutdown the inside running lanes and force the ballcarrier to run laterally—that is, parallel to the line of scrimmage. They literally spill him to the force player.

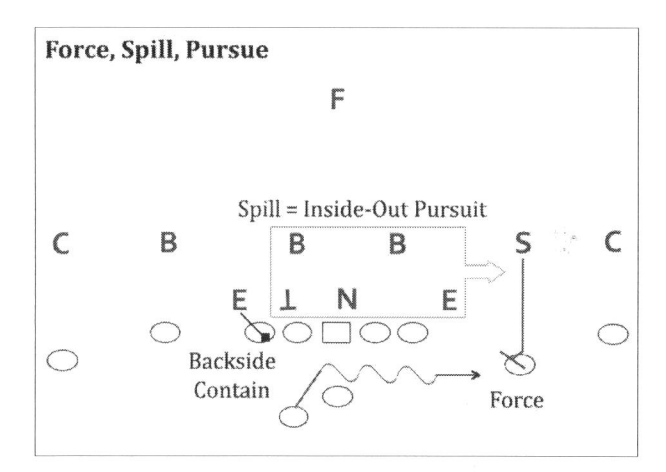

Force, Spill, Pursue

As long as the ballcarrier is running east to west, he's not gaining any yardage by running north to south. If executed as designed, the force and spill actions trap the ballcarrier in what is called the "alley," and it is there that he becomes the responsibility of the "fill" player.

The three strategies, operating in unison, contain the ballcarrier and prevent him from gaining yardage. But there's another aspect of containment that is critical to the success of any defense, and that is found on the "backside"—that side of a formation that the offense didn't attack.

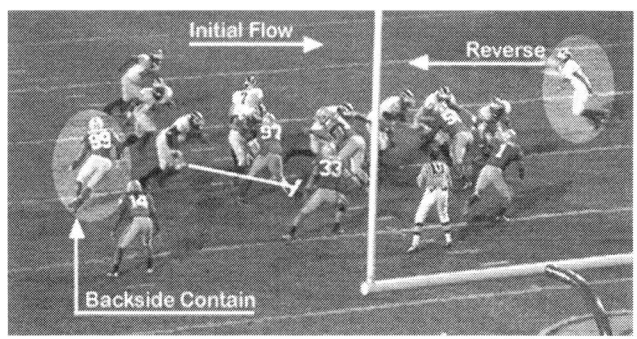

(LOC Photography)

37

The player with that job, be he the defensive end or linebacker to that side, waits to see if the play changes direction and comes back towards him. Most often that player will "replace" the offensive player positioned inside of him who, if the play is going to the opposite side of the formation, will most likely be blocking in that direction. The backside contain defender will step or slide into the space vacated by the offensive player.

His job is to prevent the ballcarrier from getting outside of him. Sometimes, though, defensive coaches will have the backside guy trail a running play going away from him as deep as the ballcarrier. The key to whatever technique is used is to keep the ballcarrier bottled up in the backfield.

Force (or contain), spill, and pursuit. Remember those three principles. To be sound—to be effecttive—all defenses must practice and master these three principles, and those that don't are doomed to fail.

A HAT IN THE CRACK

Force, contain, and pursuit are principles built into all defenses. But there are basically two ways that defenses put those principles into action on the field, and they both start with the defensive line and the gaps between the offensive linemen. Looking at how many defensive linemen there are, and how they're positioned opposite the offensive line can oftentimes tell you how the defense will defend the run.

Defenses that have a 4-man line where each is "shaded" opposite an offensive lineman—that is, partially aligned in a gap, what in coachspeak is referred to as a "hat in the crack"—is a "1-gap" defense. It's called that because one defender is assigned to one gap, and his job is to defend that gap.

In a 1-gap scheme, the defensive linemen attack their assigned gaps. Their goal is to penetrate the offensive backfield through their gap, disrupt the play and, if possible, tackle the ballcarrier. They routinely play against "half a man"—meaning they're shaded on an offensive lineman to make blocking and controlling them more difficult. They're generally selected for their speed.

In the previous photo, the defensive linemen—those players in a 3-point stance and in dark uniforms—are partially aligned on an offensive lineman and in a gap. This is what is meant by a "shade" alignment or a "hat in the crack."

The other scheme that teams sometimes use is the 2-gap. In that scheme there are generally three defensive linemen, and they're aligned "heads up" on the center and the two offensive tackles. The defensive linemen in this scheme are responsible for two gaps, the ones on either side of the offensive lineman on whom they're aligned.

Unlike their counterparts in the 1-gap scheme who don't want to stay blocked, defensive linemen in a 2-gap seek to, as coaches put it, "eat space" and keep the offensive linemen off the linebackers so they can "scrape" or flow to the ball. Their job is to engage offensive linemen, take on blocks, and read and react to where the ballcarrier is going. They're generally selected for their size and strength.

The defensive line above—those players in dark uniforms and in a 3-poount stance directly opposite an offensive lineman— are in a "heads-up" technique.

Remember that coaches, especially creative ones, are always looking for an edge. So it's not uncommon that some coaches will combine the two concepts, but in most situations you'll see the 1- and 2-gap schemes being used as described above.

DEFENDING THE PASS

Excluding the pass rush, there are three ways to defend against the pass: zone coverage, man to man, and a combination of the two, what are called combo coverages.

Zone coverages have to do with dividing the field into areas to which a defender is assigned and defends against any receiver entering it. To explain how a zone defense works, let's examine one of the more common schemes called Cover 2, with the "2" referring to the number of defenders covering the deep end of the field.

In Cover 2, there are seven defenders dropping back into coverage, while the four defensive linemen rush the passer. The seven pass defenders are arranged in two layers: the five zones, or areas of the field, under the two-deep safeties. The defenders watch the quarterback to see where the ball is thrown, and if it's in their zone, they cover the receiver attacking it.

A man-to-man scheme is as the term implies: the defender covers a specific receiver wherever he goes, not a specific zone. In this scheme the defender focuses on the receiver, not the quarterback.

Zone defenses are great versus the run because all the defenders are watching the quarterback in the backfield, and they can react quickly to a run play if they see him hand the ball off to a running back.

Man-to-man coverage is not, however, because the defenders are focused on their assigned receiver and not watching the backfield. So all too often they will react late to a run play

Often, a defensive back will position himself on the line, up close to the receiver, in what is called *press coverage.*

In this position he's not going to allow the receiver a free release from the line but will attempt to reroute him and disrupt the timing of his route by engaging him in the five yards allowed and before the ball has been thrown. The hope is that in the time it takes the receiver to escape, the pass rush will get to the quarterback and sack him.

Combo coverages, meanwhile, combine aspects of the zone with that of man-to-man schemes. A simple example of it is the Cover 2 defense discussed above, which can become a combo coverage by having the five underneath defenders play man to man while the two-deep defenders split the field into halves and play zone. In this scenario any receiver going deep will encounter double coverage because of the man assigned to him and the deep defender whose zone he attacks.

One way to determine what kind of pass coverage the defense is using is to look at the defensive backs, especially the cornerbacks positioned opposite the widest receivers. It's what quarterbacks do as well. If the cornerbacks are angled towards the formation and looking into the offensive backfield, that's a good indicator they're playing zone. If, however, their gaze is locked on the receiver, the chances are they're in man coverage.

Zone, man, and combo are the basic principles which an imaginative defensive coordinator can manipulate to create exotic schemes based on the speed of the players. At the pro level, pass coverage schemes are often complex because of their speed but also because the pros have a ton of practice time. For them, football is a full-time job.

TAMPA TWO

You will sometimes hear the term "Tampa 2" mentioned on TV. It's referring to a specific defensive scheme. Tampa—specifically the NFL's Buccaneers—is where the defense was developed, and "2" refers to the Cover 2 defense from which it evolved in response to the West Coast Offense that was running roughshod over NFL defenses back in the '80s.

The WCO was the brainchild of Bill Walsh and was made famous by Joe Montana and the San Francisco 49ers. Among its many attributes was a propensity for finding "holes" in the defense, especially behind the

middle or "Mike" linebacker. The Tampa 2 was an adjustment to the Cover 2 scheme that defended the "hole" created behind the Mike. It was developed by Monte Kiffin and Tony Dungy.

Tampa Two

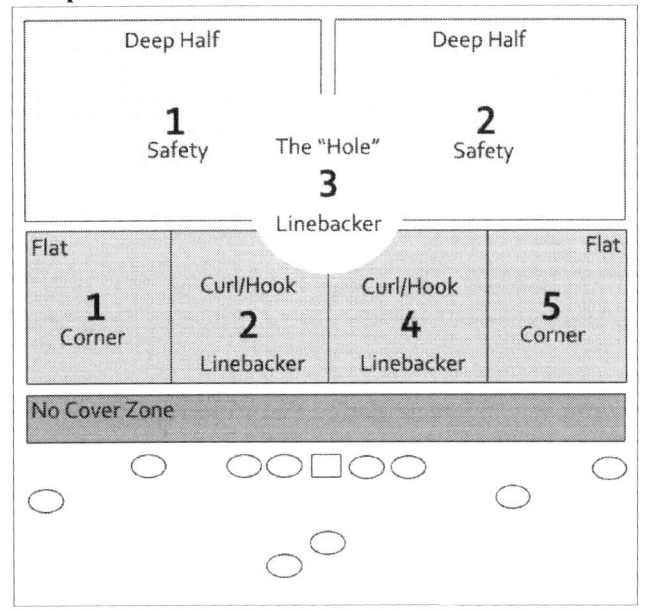

Deep Half	Deep Half
1 Safety	2 Safety

The "Hole" — 3 Linebacker

Flat	Curl/Hook	Curl/Hook	Flat
1 Corner	2 Linebacker	4 Linebacker	5 Corner

No Cover Zone

But a little research will reveal that the scheme is actually rooted in the "Steel Curtain" defenses used by the Pittsburgh Steelers back in the '70s. Basically, what the Tampa 2 did to cover the "hole" behind the middle linebacker was to drop the Mike deeper than he normally played in the Cover 2 scheme. Amazingly simple, but amazingly effective.

Because of its success, the Tampa 2 is no longer a coverage scheme that teams insert into their game plan when needed. Rather, it now serves as the base defense for some teams that, like any other base defense like the 3-4 or 4-3, can be tweaked according to an opponent's tendencies and their strengths and weaknesses.

As such, it requires specific types of skill sets at the different positions to make it work. Since all pass defense starts with the pass rush, the four defensive linemen have to be badasses and get after the quarterback in a way that allows the linebackers to drop into coverage and not blitz except in special situations.

The Tampa 2, like the Cover 2, relies on the five underneath defenders to shut down the short zones while the deep end of the field is protected by the two safeties.

BLITZING AND STUNTING

Talk about crashing the party! Blitzing and stunting are designed to do just that: break up the blocking by confusing the offensive linemen and wreak havoc in the backfield by sacking the quarterback or tackling the ballcarrier for a loss.

Blitzing is an unexpected attack from a linebacker or defensive back. But generally, a good quarterback can see it coming. The goal of any blitz is to penetrate the backfield and tackle whoever has the ball or simply disrupt the play so that no yardage—or minimal yardage—is gained.

(Massachusetts Daily Collegian)

The most lethal blitz is probably the delayed blitz where the blitzer doesn't attack at the snap of the ball but pauses a second or two to allow the blocking to adjust to any stunts. Then he attacks the opening that the design of the blitz develops. Timing in blitzing, like in life, is everything.

Stunting comes from the defensive linemen and is sometimes combined with blitzing to really confuse the blocking.

Stunting is defensive linemen trading assignments, what coaches refer to as "gap exchange" because defensive linemen, by virtue of their position in the defensive scheme, are responsible for the gaps—

those spaces between offensive linemen—in which they're aligned.

So when they exchange gaps, they're exchanging assignments and defending the gap they're attacking. The result is twists and loops and other types of choreographed maneuvers. The key, though, to any stunt or blitz is that every gap is covered and "controlled" by a defender, or the integrity of the defensive scheme breaks down.

Sometimes, too, you'll see defensive linemen suddenly shift before the ball is snapped. That is, they change their "look," forcing the offensive linemen to change their blocking scheme. This is called *stemming*.

The goal, as with stunting, is to confuse the blocking, because the offensive line only has a second or two to make any changes. Sometimes it doesn't, which creates a crease in the blocking that a defender can exploit—which is the goal of any stunt or blitz.

ZONE DOG

Sometimes, when watching a game on TV, you'll hear a commentator use the term "zone dog" or "zone blitz." They're essentially the same thing. Both are a defensive tactic intended to confuse the offensive line and sack the quarterback and quite possibly intercept a pass. To understand what a "zone dog" is, I need to give you a slice of history, along with your coffee (or is it wine?).

A "pass rush" is an attempt to sack the quarterback that comes from the defensive line. Depending upon the scheme being used, it can consist of three or four defensive linemen.

A "blitz," meanwhile, is an attack from a linebacker or a defensive back that's added to the pass rush and is sometimes unexpected. The term derives from the word "blitzkrieg"—which is the term used to describe the Nazis unexpected attack of France through Belgium at the beginning of World War II. It means "lightening war."

"Dog" is another football term for "blitz." It comes from the guy thought to have invented the "sack"—

(HoopZone)

Don "Red Dog" Ettinger—who played in the '40s. He played back when no record of sacks were kept and earned his nickname because of his tenacity and red hair.

A "zone dog" or "zone blitz" is a blitz behind which the defense is playing zone principles. It's worth mentioning because the common practice with a blitz is to play man coverage behind it. That changed sometime in the '80s when pro defenses were confronted with the precision passing attacks springing up in the league. The most lethal being that found in San Francisco under the direction of resident genius, Bill Walsh.

Dick LeBeau, the defensive coordinator for the Cincinnati Bengals back then, is commonly believed to have been the first coach to combine the blitz with a zone pass defense.

But what he actually did is refine, or improve upon a zone blitz concept put forth by Bill Arnsparger, who was Miami's defensive coordinator when they won 17 games without a loss, including a Super Bowl.

(Sports and Entertainment Nashville)   *(Amazon)*

What Arnsparger basically did was create, in his words, a "safe pressure" on the quarterback by blitzing a linebacker while dropping a defensive lineman into pass coverage. The scheme often confused the offensive line—and still does.

This led to the development of an attack called a "fire zone," which is a five-man blitz behind which the coverage is layered with three defenders underneath three defenders deep.

Example of one type of "fire zone."

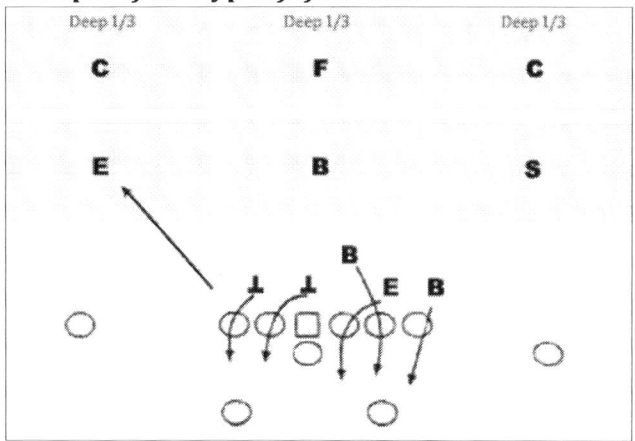

This type of attack was improved by a little tactic called "pattern matching," which is, simply put, a defender playing zone coverage until a receiver attacks the area he's covering, then he covers the receiver man-to-man.

But with pattern matching, what had started out as a blitz with a zone defense behind it, had looped back to the original concept of a blitz with a man-to-man defense behind it.

IDENTIFYING DEFENSES

Generally, defenses are identified by the number of defensive linemen they use, followed by the number of linebackers. For example, when you hear a TV commentator refer to the 4-3 defense, the four is the number of defensive linemen and the three is the number of linebackers. The four players not mentioned are the defensive backs positioned in what is most often called the "secondary."

So, using the same formula, if you hear a commentator refer to a scheme as a 3-3, you can be sure it will have three defensive linemen and three linebackers, and the five defenders not mentioned are—again—the secondary. The same can be said of a 3-4, or 4-2, etc.

Sometimes, the scheme a defense is using is not readily apparent, and that's because defenses are always disguising their intentions by aligning players in different ways. It can be confusing, and the defense hopes it is to the quarterback who, during his "pre-snap read," or analysis of the defense, is trying to determine its intentions.

So just know that, even if it doesn't look like it, any defense will consist of three levels or layers: the defensive line, the linebackers, and the defensive backs who comprise the secondary.

THE TOP TWO DEFENSES

For the longest time, football was a pretty simple game. The principal method of conveying the ball to the end zone was to run with it, so defenses were fairly simple as well. They were designed to stop the run.

As a result, fans who gathered weekly at high school fields and college stadiums across the land would be presented with schemes like the Diamond 7-1-3—seven defensive linemen, one linebacker, and what back then were called defensive halfbacks, three of them. Defenses in the infancy of football routinely used six, seven, or even eight men on the defensive line, intent on tackling the guy with the ball.

Sort of like what kids do on playgrounds.

But times have changed. So has the game. Principally, the changes have come about because of the forward pass. It's a quicker way to convey the ball to the end zone. And much more exciting. So defenses have had to catch up, and in a way, they have.

First of all, the athletes now playing the game are better trained, better conditioned, and have better skills than their predecessors. They're definitely bigger, faster, and stronger. And it's those factors—their strength and their speed—that allows defensive coordinators (DCs) to decrease the number of players on the defensive line and increase the number of players defending that parcel of turf that starts behind the linebackers and extends to the goal line—what many coaches call "the back end."

Because of the pass, defenses are now employing schemes that use three or four men along the defensive line to pressure or sack the quarterback, which respectively allows DCs to drop seven or eight men into pass coverage. There are several schemes that use three- or four-man lines, but the two most popular are the 3-4 and the 4-3.

The 3-4 has three defensive linemen and four linebackers, while the 4-3 is the opposite: four defensive linemen and three linebackers. When someone describes a defense in this manner, the first number always refers to the number of defensive linemen and the second to the number of linebackers. Whatever is left over is the number of defensive backs.

The 3-4 and the 4-3 each have seven men in the box, leaving four to defend the back end. The 3-4 and the 4-3 are the most popular "base" schemes in football—the schemes from which others emerge.

For example, you might hear of a team using a 3-3 or a 4-2 defense. No sweat. All that means is that the DC has removed one player from the defensive front so he can add a fifth defensive back to the defense. The 3-3 is actually a 3-3-5 and the 4-2 is a 4-2-5. The more players that are added to the "backend" of a defense, the fewer there are up front to defend against the run.

So the three or four defensive linemen playing up front have to be badasses. Smart guys with an attitude. Those in a three-man line are generally chosen for their size and strength. They eat up space and keep blockers off the linebackers so they can pursue the ballcarrier.

3-4 Defense

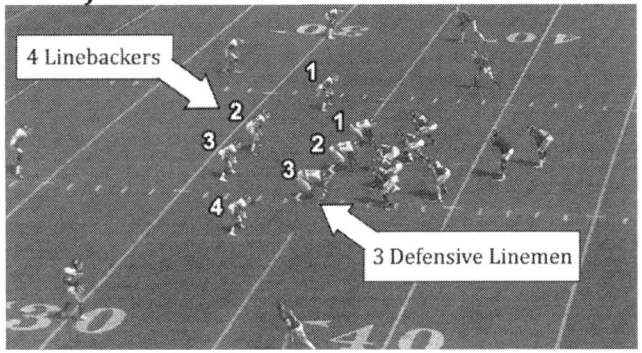

(BJ Smith)

4-3 Defense

(BJ Smith)

Those in a four-man line are chosen for their speed, their quickness off the ball, because they're penetrators. They're looking to get into the backfield and disrupt the play, if not tackle the ballcarrier. Two different strategies, two different types of defensive linemen. (See the slice: A Hat in the Crack*)*

Speed is the key. Players are recruited to college for their speed. And so are the handful that are drafted into the pros. The faster the defensive players are, the more creative a DC can be—the more sophisticated. But the same can be said of an offense, which makes the back and forth that regularly occurs in a game all the more exciting to watch.

SPECIAL TEAMS

Lou Holtz, a former college coach who won a bunch of games at different schools and a national championship at Notre Dame, once advised that "... if you want to win an away game, you better pack your defense and special teams."

(Amazon)

He included special teams in his luggage not simply because of the field goals or extra points they can produce, but because of how punting and kick-offs can impact a game in terms of field position and sudden changes in momentum.

A long return can put a team in an excellent position to score, while a long run to the end zone can alter the character of a game and a team's level of motivation. The team that scored can be inspired, while the team that allowed it can be demoralized.

Coaches who want to win take special teams seriously. It's one-third of their game plan—and not the last third. It is said that defense wins championships, but it can be argued that special teams often wins games.

Kick-off Team—refers to the 11 players who line up to kick the ball to their opponent to begin play at the start of a game, the second half, or after a score. Where the ball is kicked from varies according to the level of competition. In the pros the ball is kicked from the kicking team's 35-yard line.

(GameSpot)

If the ball goes into the end zone and is recovered by a member of the kicking team, it's a touchdown. But if the ball goes beyond the end zone or is caught by the return man and downed in the end zone, it's called a *touchback*, and in the NFL the ball is spotted at the 25-yard line for the receiving team's offense to begin play.

Sometimes, when a team is losing and needs to gain possession of the ball again after scoring, the kick-off team will attempt an onside kick. The rule during a kick-off is that once the ball travels ten yards, or is touched by a member of the receiving team, it's fair game to be recovered by any member of the kick-off team.

So the ball is squibbed at an angle into the front row of players on the receiving team to travel the required ten yards, with the hope that it'll bounce high into the air, making it difficult to handle and increasing the chances that someone on the kick-off team can regain possession of the ball.

Onside Kick— Because the ball is a "free ball" once it travels ten yards in a kick-off or touches someone on the receiving team, any member of the kicking team can recover it, and that's why we have "onside kicks."

An onside kick can be executed during any kick-off but is most often seen when the kicking team is losing in the closing minutes of a game and needs to regain possession of the ball.

Sometimes, it's a surprise tactic, but most of the time you'll know something's up by the arrangement of the players on the kicking team and how the receiving team forms up anticipating a short kick. In this situation the coaches of the receiving team will send out their "good hands" team, which consists of players who are accustomed to handling the ball.

(LOC Photography)

The most common type of onside kick is the "high-bounce" kick. The kicker kicks the ball above its centerline, causing it to flip end over end, until during one rotation it bounces high into the air and everyone scrambles for the ball.

Onside Kick: mishandled high bounce

(Sheboygan Press)

Kick Return Team—refers to the 11 players deployed opposite the kick-off team who receive any kick-off. Once the ball is kicked they rush downfield to tackle the ballcarrier.

Good Hands Team—see Onside Kick.

Punt Team—refers to the 11 players who kick the ball on 4th down. It includes a specialist in hiking the ball (long-snapper) and a punter, who is a kicker who specializes in punting the ball—that is kick the ball to the opposing team when the offense has failed to earn a first down.

Oftentimes, if the punt team is at midfield, the punter will attempt to angle the kick toward the sideline, near the goal line, to prevent a return and have the opposing team start its offensive series with its back to its own end zone.

FOOTBALL FOR MOMS AND SWEETHEARTS

(Danny Wild)

Or, and there's always an "or," he will kick it a mile high to give the punt team—who are now the defenders—time to get under the kick and tackle the return man before he gets started. There's a strategy to everything that teams and coaches do.

Be aware, too, that sometimes the punt team will fake a punt and run a play in an attempt to gain the yardage needed for a first down.

Punt Return Team—refers to the 11 players who receive the punt. Once the ball is kicked, they become the offensive team. The object of the return's design is to score or gain as much yardage as possible.

(SB Nation)

Often, you'll see the return man—the player designated to catch the ball and run with it—settle under a high kick and wave his arm over his head. That's the signal for a fair catch. That means no defender can tackle him or interfere with his attempt to catch the ball. It also means he can't advance the ball.

If the return man muffs the catch, meaning he drops it, any member of the punt team can recover it but not return it. But if the return man catches the ball and runs with it, then fumbles the ball, the ball can be picked up and returned to the punt team's end zone.

Muffed Punt

(Jacksonville.com)

Field Goal—is kicking the ball between the uprights of the goal posts. The field goal can be kicked at any time during an offensive series, but it is generally done during a fourth down and only when the offense is within the kicker's range. If good, the offense is awarded three points. If not, the defense gets the ball where it was spotted before the failed kick.

(DuckDuckGo)

Point After Touchdown (PAT)—the point after touchdown, or PAT, is kicked after a touchdown has been scored. The NFL, to make it more challenging, has moved the kick back to the 15-yard line which, when you include the ten yards in the end zone, makes the kick 25 yards long.

Still pretty much a gimme for a pro kicker, but anything can happen—and sometimes does. The kick, if good, is worth one point.

Another type of PAT is the two-point conversion. After scoring a touchdown, teams have the option to attempt a two-point conversion instead of kicking the ball. The conversion attempt is an offensive play in which the offense can either pass the ball into the end zone for two points or run it in.

If, however, the defense manages to wrangle the ball from the offense, they can run it back to their end zone and score two points.

SWINGING GATE

Sometimes, after a team has scored a touchdown, they'll line up in an exotic formation in which the bulk of the team is positioned to one side of the field, while the remaining three or four players are abandoned to its middle. Most often, what you're seeing is a unique tactic called the Swinging Gate, as depicted in the photo below.

(Scout.com)

The idea is to see what the defense does. As with any exotic formation, the intent is to confuse the defense. Most often, the strategy is to attack wherever a mismatch in numbers appears, be it opposite the offensive line at the top, or with the individual players below.

But even when there isn't a mismatch in numbers, there are a variety of plays that can be run from the Swinging Gate, including throwing a pass to the center who, in this formation, is an eligible receiver. But as with any offensive formation, the swinging gate must be legal.

That is, it must have seven players on the line and only four in the backfield. And, to be an eligible receiver, *the end man on either side of the line—like the center—cannot be "covered." That means that no one can be positioned outside of him on the same line.*

The Swinging Gate can be used in any situation, but it is primarily used to score two points after a touchdown, instead of kicking for one.

Often though, when offenses don't get the mismatch they seek, they'll shift and regroup opposite the goalpost and kick the ball for the one point. The tactic, which dates back to the '30s, is still used by many high school and college teams.

SCORING

Touchdown—equals six points if the ball is carried or passed into the end zone by a member of the team with possession of the ball. That means, if the defense recovers a fumble or intercepts a pass, they now have possession of the ball and can carry it into their end zone.

Field Goal—equals three points, which are awarded to the offense if its placekicker kicks the ball between the uprights of the goalposts.

(SB Nation)

Point After Touchdown (PAT)—equals one point if the ball is kicked between the uprights on the goalpost or two if the ball is carried into or caught in the end zone.

Safety—equals two points awarded to the defense when the ballcarrier, either a running back or the quarterback, is tackled in his own end zone. Then, as if to add salt to the wound, the offense is required to surrender possession of the ball by kicking it from its 20-yard line to the defense's kick-off return team.

FOOTBALL FOR MOMS AND SWEETHEARTS

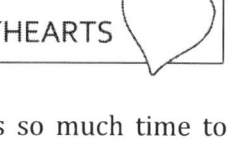

The upside down guy in the photo above is the quarterback, and he's in possession of the ball, and he's in the end zone. In any other level of competition, this would be an automatic safety because he's down, but not in the NFL. For it to be a safety in the NFL, a defensive player—like #94—has to at least touch the quarterback while he's in this predicament for him to be considered "down" or tackled.

TIME

In the pros and college, football games are divided into two halves, comprised of two 15-minute quarters each. Twelves minutes in high school. In between the two halves is a 15-minute half-time, during which teams catch their breath and coaching staffs make adjust-ments to their game plan. That only adds up to an hour-and-fifteen minutes, so why are foot-ball games so long?

Games are long because the clock stops for different reasons, especially if you're watching the game on TV. The networks have to make their money, so there are TV time-outs that can be added to the following list of reasons that the game clock stops:

—when a timeout is called,
—on a penalty,
—when the ballcarrier or the ball goes out of bounds,
—when a team scores,
—after a change of possession,
—after an incomplete pass,
—when the quarterback spikes the ball because it is an incomplete pass,
—when a player is injured,
—when there's a measurement for a first down,
—at the end of a quarter,
—in the pros, when the two-minute warning is given,
—and in college and high school, when a first down is made.

After a play an offense only has so much time to huddle—if they do—and form up at the line to initiate another play. If play has stopped for any of the reasons listed above, the offense has 25 seconds.

If, however, play hasn't been stopped, they have 40 seconds from the end of the previous play. What you often see, though, are teams not huddling but quickly forming at the line to get a play off in less than 15 seconds. The idea is to speed up the game, and there are four good reasons for it:

—to exhaust the defense,
—to prevent the defense from substituting players,
—to force defenses to use conservative schemes,
—and to increase the number of plays the offense can run in a game, thus increasing their chances of scoring a lot of points.

Clock management is a critical aspect of any game-day strategy. How coaches use the time remaining to them at the end of the first half, or at the end of the second half in a close game, will often determine the outcome of the game.

Time is such a precious commodity that some coaches don't allow players to call time-outs in the second half, particularly in the pros where time-outs are used to challenge a referee's call. If the coach is right and the referee wrong, the team doesn't lose the time-out.

But if the coach is wrong, then his team loses that time out. In this context, then, football is not only a game of inches but of 20/20 vision as well. Coaches need to be sure about what they saw before they challenge an official's call.

Clock management in critical situations has been described as "giving birth," but I'm not sure how football coaches would know about that. Our wives, for sure. But us? Not really. And yet, the decision-making process in the closing seconds of an intense, closely-fought game between rivals can mirror the pressure-packed environment of a hospital's busy ER where life-and-death choices are made in milli-seconds.

For a coach along the sideline, the decision-making process can feel like that, especially in big-money games like the Super Bowl. But for you, the spectator, it begins with three simple questions: who's winning, by how much, and how much time is left.

If the team in the lead is in possession of the ball, they will want to eat up as much time as they can. They will be slow to huddle, slow to assemble at the line, and slow to snap the ball, appearing to nap until only one or two seconds remain on the play clock, at which point the ball is snapped.

Killing Time: the huddle

(Kevin McGuire)

The play-calling will be simple. Chances are they will run the ball because the clock doesn't stop after the ballcarrier has been tackled. They will want to stay inbounds, too, because the clock stops if the ball-carrier goes out of bounds.

Something they don't want to happen.

To retain possession of the ball, though, they may have to throw the ball to gain a first down, so it will be a safe and easy throw that can be caught and advanced, because an incomplete pass will stop the clock. The goal is to retain possession of the ball and waste time. They will call no time-outs, or at least they shouldn't.

If, however, the team on offense is losing, they will want to save time. Uptempo, no-huddle teams do that even when they're not losing, but teams using traditional offensive schemes will roll out their "two-minute offense," which is a package of plays designed and practiced just for this situation.

Where teams wanting to waste time will run the ball, teams wanting to save time will throw it because the clock stops on an incomplete pass. But more importantly, in college and high school games, the clock stops when the offense gains a first down.

Often a team wanting to save time will rush to the line after a play, and after being set for one count, the quarterback will receive the snap and "spike" the ball—that is, throw it into the ground. The reason is simple: it saves time because it's an incomplete pass and will stop the clock. So will running out of bounds. In either case the offense has 25 seconds to regroup and choose what play to use next, as it might be the last play in the game.

On the other side of the line, the defense, wanting to save time for the offense, will call time-outs. It will look to "tackle the ball"—that is, strip the ball from the ballcarrier's grasp and create a fumble. It will anticipate that the offense will run the ball, so it will use schemes that are designed to shut down the run, to force the offense into a fourth down situation in which it has to surrender possession of the ball by punting it to the defense.

Stripping the Ball

In the photo above, a defensive player (#12) is attempting to strip the ball from the ballcarrier (#23). Stripping the ball is a tactic routinely practiced by teams. *(Photo AJC.com)*

The strategies are numerous. The tactics, too. The field situation and the time remaining on the clock will determine which approach the team winning and the team losing will use. One thing's for sure though, when you see a team's offense line up in the "victory" formation, the outcome of the game has been decided.

(Wikipedia)

48

FOOTBALL FOR MOMS AND SWEETHEARTS

Overtime

In the pros it's called "sudden death." The game is played as if there is a fifth quarter. The first team to scores, wins.

In college and high school, teams take turns attempting to score from the defense's 25-yard line. From there the game is played until the offense scores or is stopped on fourth down or through a turnover. Then the other team gets its shot from the 25-yard line. If it scores more than its opponent, it wins. If it doesn't, it loses. If the teams tie, they repeat the procedure until one teams wins.

THE FIELD AND ITS FEATURES

(TP Reed)

A football field is 120 yards long and 53-1/3 yards wide. That includes the 10 yards at either end of the field that constitute the end zones which, when entered by a ballcarrier, result in a touchdown. Distinctive features are:

—A "sideline" runs the length of the field on either side. It's six feet wide and is considered out of bounds.

(CapSam)

—The end zone is where the scoring occurs. They are two, and they're located at either end of the field. They're as wide as the field, and are ten yards deep. There are brightly-colored pylons—usually orange or yellow—at each corner. The end zone behind a team is the one they'll defend, while the one in front of them is the end zone they seek to penetrate to score.

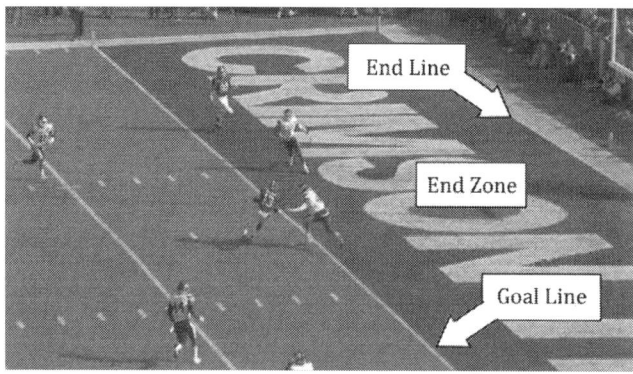

(LOC Photography)

—The "goal line" is at the front of each end zone. It's eight inches wide and extends from sideline to sideline. When TV commentators are talking about touch-downs, you might hear them use the phrase "breaks the plane of the goal line." The phrase refers to when any part of the ball crosses the goal line, and not the guy carrying the ball. That's when a touchdown is scored.

—At the back of the end zones are "end lines." They're six feet wide and are boundary lines that connect the two sidelines. It's the end lines and sidelines that create the field's rectangular shape. Two pylons flank the end of the end line.

—Yard lines are solid white lines that appear on the field every five yards. They extend from sideline to sideline. The yard lines at ten-yard intervals are numbered and generally thicker. The numbers start with "10" at the 10-yard line and progress to the 50-yard line at the center of the field, which divides the field into two halves, then goes backward to the 10-yard line at the opposite end of the field.

—"Hashmarks" are the tiny, white lines between the yard lines on either side of the field. They're one yard long and mark each yard on the field. They are the inbound lines. When the ballcarrier goes out of bounds, the ball is spotted by the referees at the nearest hashmark on that side of the field. But when the ballcarrier is tackled between the hashmarks, the ball is spotted where he was downed.

49

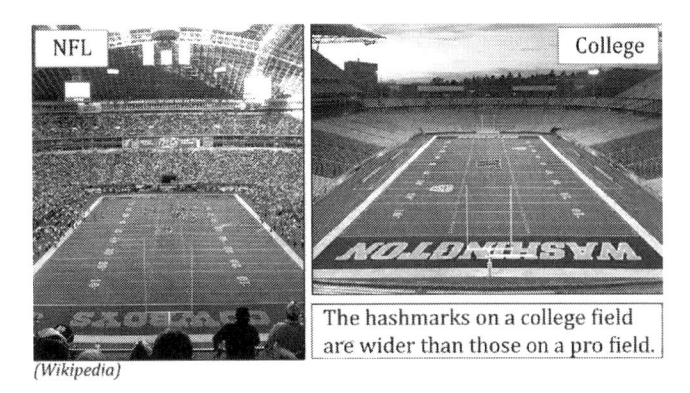

FOOTBALL FOR MOMS AND SWEETHEARTS

The hashmarks on a college field are wider than those on a pro field.
(Wikipedia)

In the pros, the hashmarks are 70 feet, 9 inches from the sideline. They're as wide apart as the goalposts at the back of each end zone: 18 feet, 6 inches.

In college and high school, though, the hashmarks are 60 feet from the sideline and wider than the goalposts. This makes kicking field goals in college or high school more difficult than in the pros because the closer the ball is to the end zone, the more severe the angle of the kick is.

The pro game, though, is more balanced because the hashmarks are closer together. When the ball is spotted at one hashmark, there's almost an equal amount of open grass on either side to attack.

Effects of Hashmarks on an NFL Field

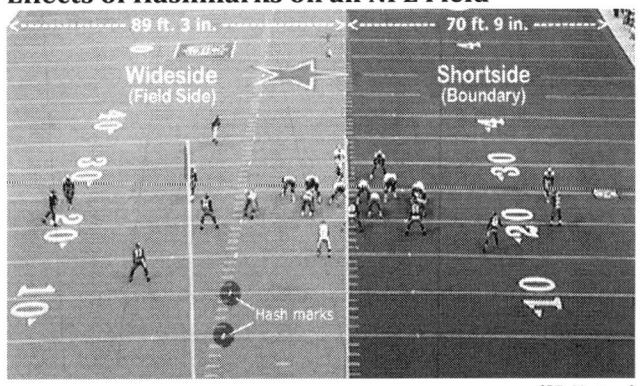

(SB Nation)

Not so in college and high school where the hashmarks are wider apart so that when the ball is spotted there, it creates a "wideside" and "shortside" of the field—what coaches call the "field side" and "boundary" respectively.

For example, there's more "open grass" to the wideside, so there's more area for the offense to attack and more for the defense to defend. So you might see the offense throwing more often into the field side rather than the boundary.

Effects of Hashmarks on a College Field

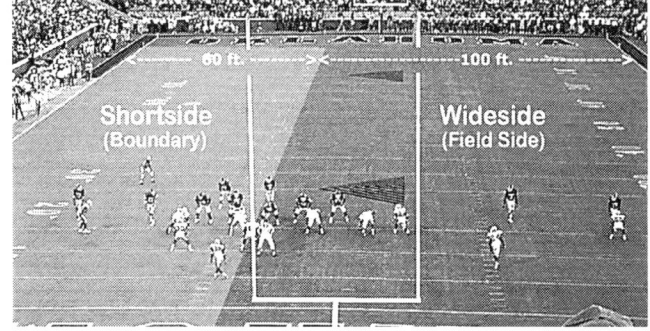

(OUInsider Forum)

A Brief History of Hashmarks

Back in the day there were no hashmarks and very few rules. The next offensive play started where the previous ended. If the ballcarrier was tackled close to the sideline, the spot was spotted close to the sideline.

(YouTube)

It was college football that introduced the hashmark in 1933 when it learned that teams were wasting plays to gain better field position. And it was the NFL who moved the hashmarks 20 yards inside of the sideline in 1945 which, when the ball was spotted for play, clearly divided the field into a "wideside" and a "shortside." What coaches call the "field side" and the "boundary."

—Goalposts are found at the back of each end zone at either end of the field. The uprights in the pros are as wide as the hashmarks on the field: 18 feet, 6 inches. In college, the uprights are the same width as the pros, but college hashmarks are wider, making field goals difficult to kick the closer the kicker is to the goalposts.

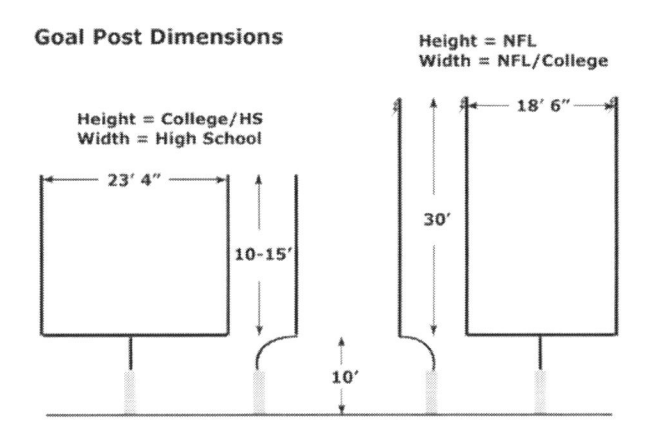

FOOTBALL FOR MOMS AND SWEETHEARTS

Goal Post Dimensions

Height = College/HS
Width = High School
23' 4"
10-15'

Height = NFL
Width = NFL/College
18' 6"
30'
10'

High school goalposts are 23 feet, 4 inches wide, making field goals much easier to kick. The cross bar at all levels is ten feet off the ground, but the posts in the pros are an additional 20 feet high. At the top of each upright is a brightly colored flag so that kickers can gauge the strength and direction of any wind.

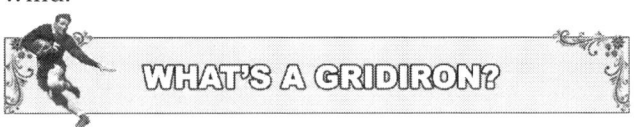

WHAT'S A GRIDIRON?

It's not often heard anymore, but football fields were routinely called a "gridiron" because, as was reported in a 1911 copy of Outdoor Sports and Games, *"...The lines on a football field [made] a checkerboard effect and [gave] to the field the name of "gridiron." Eventually, the term came to mean the game itself, even though the grid system of marking the field was later replaced by yard lines.*

Gridiron: Syracuse University 1910

(Onondaga County Library)

PLAYER NUMBERS

Uniform numbers must be worn by all players for identification purposes by officials, fans, and TV commentators. The numbers are on the front and back, and TV numbers, if any, are generally on the sleeves or shoulders.

In most cases, especially in college and the pros, specific numbers are worn according to the position of the player. Colleges and the pros can afford to buy new jerseys for new players who are a different size than their predecessor, but high schools and youth organizations cannot. They will try to conform to the rules, but will assign jerseys according to size.

Under current rules, players must wear a number between 1 and 99, and no two players on the same team can wear the same number on the field at the same time. In the NFL, the range of uniform numbers is broken down by position:

01–19: by rule for quarterbacks, punters, and place-kickers,
20–49: by rule-running backs and defensive backs,
50–59: customary for centers and linebackers,
60–79: offensive linemen/some defensive linemen,
10–19 or 80–89: by rule-wide receivers,
80–89 (by rule) and 40–49 (optional): tight ends,
90–99: some defensive ends and linebackers.

Players wearing a number between 50-79 are ineligible to cross the line of scrimmage and catch a pass unless the player is, by formation, eligible to do so, meaning he is one of the end men on either side of the line, he is uncovered, and he has reported to the official that he will be eligible.

SCOREBOARD

Scoreboards, like that shown below, will generally report the score, the time remaining in the quarter, what quarter it is, the number of time-outs remaining to a team (each team gets three per half), the down-and-distance situation, and where on the field the ball is spotted.

The scoreboard on the next page is what is commonly seen at high school and youth football games. The score-board in most stadiums, especially pro

51

and college, will be huge and positioned at one end of the field—usually where the flag pole is located—and is easily viewed by everyone in the stadium.

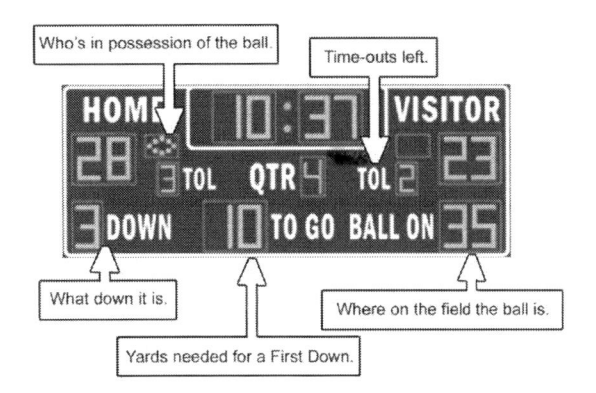

In games broadcast on TV, the network will provide a small scoreboard that, in most cases, reports the same information but is configured differently so it fits on the screen, probably in a corner where it does not interfere with your view of the game.

CHAIN CREW

The chain crew is three guys who keep track of the down-and-distance markers along the sideline. In the first half they're on the home team's sideline, and in the second, they're on the visiting teams sideline. They're most often known as the "chain gang" because of the ten yards of metal chain linking the yard markers together.

The chain crew operate three vertical poles, as shown in the picture below. The yard markers show what yard line the offensive series started and where it must go to earn another "first down." The third pole identifies where the ball is currently spotted and, at it's top, what down it is.

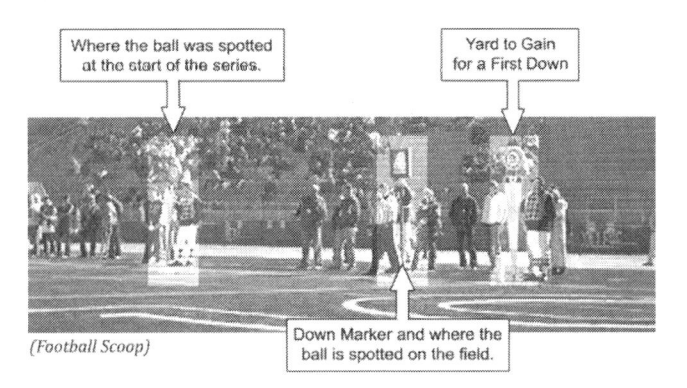

(Football Scoop)

The crew is under the supervision of the linesman, who let's them know the field situation. The crew themselves is not involved in any decisions. But they're often asked to make key measurements in a game where inches often decide the outcome. In the case of the chain gang, their accuracy is critical as, oftentimes during an official measurement, the offense is either inches short of the first down line or inches past it.

COMMON RULE VIOLATIONS

Note: To simplify your introduction to the game's most common infractions and their penalties, I have relied on the rules used by the National Football League (NFL). Keep in mind, too, that most defensive penalties result in a first down because of their distance.

Also, a little something common to all infractions is the "half the distance to the goal" effect. How that works is that once the ball is inside the 20-yard line, the penalty—that is, the yardage lost—is assessed so that no penalty can move the ball more than "half the distance" toward the offending team's goal line.

The three exceptions are: defensive pass interference, intentional grounding, and offensive holding. As for the latter, offensive holding, if it occurs within the offensive team's own end zone, it results in an automatic safety.

Ball, the—the ball is made up of an inflated urethane bladder that's enclosed in a pebble grained, leather case without corrugations of any kind. It shall have the form of a prolate spheroid and the size and weight shall be: long axis, 11 to 11¼ inches; long circumference, 28 to 28½ inches; short circumference, 21 to 21¼ inches; weight, 14 to 15 ounces.

Block in the Back—refers to a player on the kick-off or punt return team who blocks a defender above the waist and in the back. It's illegal and results in a ten-yard penalty from the spot of the foul or half the distance to the goal line if the foul occurred inside the 20-yard line.

FOOTBALL FOR MOMS AND SWEETHEARTS

Block in the Back
(DateHookUp.com)

Chop Block—is an illegal and dangerous block performed by two offensive players on one defender. One offensive player "posts" the defender—meaning he engages the defender above the waist—while the second offensive player drives into his legs. The chop block can cause serious injury, which is why it's illegal. Penalty: loss of 15 yards.

(FootballScoop.com)
Chop Block

Delay of Game—refers to any action that impedes or "delays" the initiation of the next play. The penalty can be assessed to either team. Penalty: loss of five yards for the offending team.

Encroachment—occurs when a defensive player crosses the neutral zone and makes contact with an offensive player. Penalty: loss of five yards.

Facemask—grabbing the facemask of an opposing player to either tackle or block him. Penalty: loss of 15 yards if the offense involves twisting the helmet and the head inside. Loss of five yards if the infraction is incidental. 
(Wikipedia)

False Start—despite all the movement you see before the offense settles in at the line of scrimmage, like offensive linemen pointing at defenders, the offense is required to be "set"—meaning motionless—before the ball is snapped. A false start is when an offensive player moves, giving the impression that the play has started. Defensive players are not required to be set. They can move all they want but cannot cross the line. Penalty: loss of five yards.

Holding (Defensive or Offensive)—is grabbing a player other than the ballcarrier to hinder his advance or fight off an attempt to be blocked or covered by a defender.

Defensive linemen are taught to grab an offensive linemen to "shed" them—meaning move them—but it can't be sustained. They have to grab them, toss them aside, then go. They can't hold on. Neither can offensive linemen. Penalty: loss of ten yards, except if the offense occurs in the offense's end zone, then the defense is awarded a safety.

(Nick Lucero)
Holding

Horse Collar—occurs when a defender grabs the inside of a ballcarrier's shoulder pads at the neck and jerks him to the ground. The key phrase here is "inside the shoulder pads," as players sometimes grab the jersey. Penalty: loss of 15 yards.

(SB Nation)

53

Illegal Formation—is an offensive penalty. It occurs when the offense has fewer than seven players on the line, which means there are more than four in the backfield. Penalty: loss of five yards.

Illegal Participation—can apply to both teams and is different from illegal substitution because the word "participation" means that the illegal 12th player has played during a down. Penalty: loss of 15 yards.

Illegal Motion—is an offensive penalty. It occurs when the player in motion moves toward or crosses the line of scrimmage before the snap. Penalty: loss of five yards.

Illegal Shift—is an offensive penalty that occurs when a player who is in motion was not set for one count before the snap or when more than one player goes in motion before the snap. Penalty: loss of five yards.

Illegal Substitution—can occur with either team. It's simply when a team has too many players on the field. An offense can be penalized for having 12 players in the huddle at any time between when a huddle is formed and breaks.

The defense can be called if it has 12 players on the field at the snap of the ball, even if one of those players is trying desperately to leave the field. Penalty: loss of five yards and the down is replayed. (See Illegal Participation.)

Ineligible Receiver Downfield—is an offensive foul because it refers to an offensive lineman who has crossed the line of scrimmage to block someone during a pass play in which the ball has been thrown down-field. Offensive linemen are ineligible to catch a pass because they're not lined up in the backfield and they're not the end man on either side of the line.

The exception is the tackle-eligible play in which, in the formation's design, an offensive tackle *is* the end man and he has alerted officials that he's going out for a pass. It should be noted, too, that there is no "screen pass" exception in the NFL, like there is in college, where offensive linemen can block down-field if the pass is thrown *behind* the line. Penalty: loss of five yards.

Intentional Grounding—occurs when the quarterback is about to be sacked and to prevent it, he "intentionally" throws the ball into the ground to keep from losing yardage or, in some situations, to save time. This can be easily confused with "spiking" the ball, which occurs when the quarterback purposely throws the ball into the ground to stop the clock.

The rule allowing that says, "... a player [the quarterback] under center is permitted to stop the game clock *legally* to save time if, immediately upon receiving the snap, he begins a continuous throwing motion and throws the ball directly into the ground."

The quarterback is clearly not doing that when he's trying to keep from losing yardage. Penalty: loss of five yards from the spot of the foul, plus loss of the down.

The quarterback being tackled in the end zone above is attempting to prevent a "safety" being awarded the defense by intentionally grounding the ball. *(Buffalo News)*

Neutral Zone Infraction—occurs when a defensive player enters the neutral zone before the ball is snapped and causes an offensive player to false start. Penalty: loss of five yards.

Offsides—a player is offsides when any part of his body is beyond his line of scrimmage or free-kick line during a kick-off when the ball is snapped or kicked. It's not a rule in the NFL. See Encroachment. Penalty: loss of five yards.

Pass Interference—occurs during a pass play. It's when the defender makes "intentional" contact with the intended receiver after the ball has been thrown, and before it has been caught, so as to prevent the completion of the pass. Penalty: loss of 15 yards. It doesn't make any difference if the violation was committed in the end zone.

FOOTBALL FOR MOMS AND SWEETHEARTS

Often a defender who has been beaten will purposely interfere with a receiver's attempt to catch a pass because the penalty yardage is less then what the receiver would gain if he caught the ball.

(The Cheat Sheet)

Personal Foul—is a catch-all offense that covers safety-related infractions like unnecessary roughness, hitting the ballcarrier out of bounds, etc. Penalty: loss of 15 yards for the offending team. Ejection if the offense is deemed flagrant.

Roughing the Kicker—is a special teams infraction. It occurs when a defender misses blocking a kick and ends up tackling or running into the kicker, who is unprotected. The offense includes the holder during a placekick attempt. Penalty: loss of 15 yards by the defense and an automatic first down. Running into the kicker, which is a lesser offense, results in a loss of five yards.

Roughing the Passer—occurs when a defender slams the quarterback to the ground after he has thrown the ball. Even a hand to the facemask can be considered hitting above the shoulders, which is not allowed or tolerated. Penalty: offense is awarded 15 yards—which can be added to whatever yardage was gained by the play during which the infraction occurred—and an automatic first down.

Roughing the Kicker   **Roughing the Passer**

(Owl.ly)   *(Niner Nation)*

Spearing—is contacting an opponent with the helmet. The offending player can be either on the offense or defense, as the purpose for the rule is to prevent a neck injury to the player making the contact. Penalty: loss of 15 yards for the offending team, plus an automatic first down if committed by the defense.

Spearing

(California Golden Blogs)   **Targeting** = helmet to helmet.

Targeting—occurs when a defensive player "targets" a defenseless offensive player who has the ball by hitting him "forcefully" above the neck or by making helmet-to-helmet contact using the crown of the helmet. This infraction is reviewable by video. Penalty: the offense is awarded 15 yards, and if intentional, the offending player is ejected from the game.

Unnecessary Roughness—is a personal foul in which a player uses excessive force to block or tackle another player beyond what is necessary. Piling on, hitting a player who is out of bounds, grabbing a player by his facemask or collar, or head-butting are all forms of unnecessary roughness. These penalties are safety-related because of the great risk of injury. Penalty: loss of 15 yards.

(BAGnewsNotes)

COMMON TV TERMS

55

FOOTBALL FOR MOMS AND SWEETHEARTS

The language of football is rich and varied—and very descriptive. Compiling it all would take a book unto itself, so I didn't. Instead, I identified key terms and expressions routinely used by TV commentators to describe the action that will help you understand and enjoy the game. What is not here will become known to you the more you watch the game and apply what you learn in this book.

1-Gap or **2-Gap Defense**—refer to the slice under *Identifying Defenses*.

1-High or **2-High Safeties**—refers to the number of defensive backs, routinely the "safeties," who are positioned in the deepest part of the secondary. In a 1-high alignment, there's one, and in a 2-high, there are two. When you see one, that usually means the defense is playing man-to-man coverage beneath him and maybe thinking about blitzing.

(BJ Smith)

If there are two safeties, they split the deep end of the field into halves and each is responsible for defending any receiver who enters his half of the field. The defense underneath can be playing man-to-man or zone coverage.

1-on-1 Coverage—is coachspeak for man-to-man pass defense, meaning one pass defender is assigned to one receiver.

Backside (Playside)—is the side of an offensive formation that the offense is not attacking. Conversely, the playside is the side being attacked.

(Ben Ostrander)

Behind the Chains—see *Staying Ahead of the Chains*.

Blindside—is the side of the field the quarterback can't see as he sets up to throw the ball. Defenses position their fastest and best pass rusher on that side of a formation which is commonly called the "blindside". Offenses counter by putting their best pass blocker opposite that particular rusher which is why he is generally the highest paid lineman..

(Factory of Sadness)

Blitz—see the section *Stunting and Blitzing*.

Bomb, the—refers to a long pass. A very long pass. The idea is to score and, failing that, to stretch a defense vertically, meaning toward the end zone. If a defense knows that an offense will go long, it's less likely to play it close to the line of scrimmage, thus exposing itself to attack from run plays and to passes underneath the deep zones.

Bootleg—is an offensive play with multiple personalities. It's a play-action pass, a misdirection play, and a kind of option play all coming off the action of a running play. Play action gets the bootleg started. It's what causes the defense to initially attack in the wrong direction.

The quarterback fakes a hand-off to a running back going to one side of the formation, which an aggressive defense will likely overpursue. That's followed immediately by misdirection when, concealing the ball, the quarterback rolls out opposite the run fake and into the perimeter, where he has the option to either pass or run, depending upon how the "force" defender there reacts to his sudden appearance with the ball.

If the defender attacks, the quarterback can throw the ball to one of the receivers the play design has stacked to that side of the field. But if the defender lays back and covers the pass, the quarterback can run.

The key to any bootleg, though, is the running play upon which it is based. It has to be working in order for the defense to be fooled by the run fake, especially if the offense proposes to run a type of bootleg called a "naked." A naked simply means that the quarterback has no protection. The contain defender—usually a defensive end or linebacker—is not blocked, because the offense anticipates that he will overreact to flow away from him and give up contain by pursuing in the direction of the fake.

In the bootleg below, the quarterback (#6) is being forced to throw to the only open receiver by the "force" defender (#1).

(LOC Photography)

Boundary (Shortside)—when the ballcarrier goes out of bounds, the ball is spotted at the nearest hashmark. Hashmarks are those short white lines that are on either side of the field and run parallel to the sideline. They're individual yard markers. What that does, though, is make one side of the field wider than the other, especially in college and high school. Coaches refer to the shortside as the "boundary" and the wideside as the "field side."

(OUInsider Forum)

Bracket Coverage—see *Double Coverage*.

Breaking Contain—describes situations in which a ballcarrier has escaped the backfield by getting outside the "contain" defender at the edge of an offensive formation or the contain defender in a kick or punt coverage scheme.

Busted Coverage—refers to a pass defense that, due to a missed assignment by one of the defenders, has allowed an offensive receiver to get wide open.

Checkdown—refers to the pass thrown to a receiver who, by the play's design, is the safety valve for the quarterback to throw to when no one else is open. The longer a quarterback takes to go through his pass progression—that is, the process by which he checks receivers in a certain sequence to see who is open—the greater chance the pass rush has to sack him. The checkdown prevents this.

Checkout—is the new term for an audible. It's what the quarterback is doing when he changes the offense's play at the line of scrimmage to a play that will work versus the scheme the defense is using. He's "checking out" of a bad play and into a good one.

Coffin Corner—refers to an area of the field that punt teams some-times target with a punt to place their opponent in bad field position. The "coffin corner" is formed where the goal line intersects the sideline. The tactic seeks to have the ball go out of bounds so there is no return and to have their opponent start their offensive series with their backs to their own end zone. The term is reportedly adopted from the "coffin corner" found in Victorian homes.

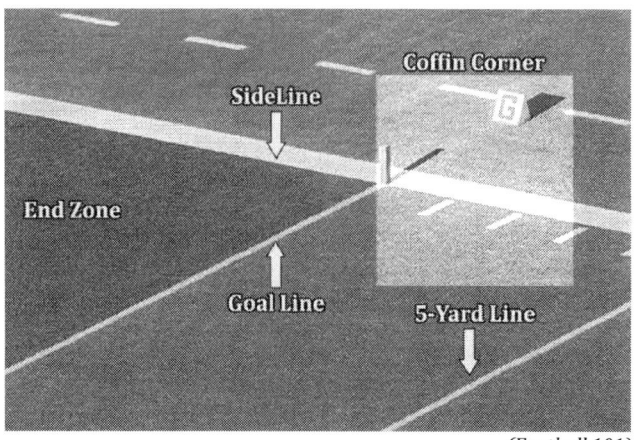

(Football 101)

Combo Coverage—refers to a pass defense that combines both zone and man-to-man principles. *(See Defending the Pass.)*

Coming Off the Edge—refers to the "heat" or pressure on the quarterback that comes from a speedy edge defender. *(See Edge Defender)*

Contain—see the section *Defending the Run*.

Coverage Beaters—refers to pass patterns that are designed to defeat specific types of pass defenses.

Coverage Sack—is a sack of the quarterback that happens because the pass defense or "coverage" is so tight that the quarterback has no one to throw to. He simply runs out of time and the pass rush catches him.

Coverage Shell—think of a pass defense in three layers: the pass rush, the underneath coverage—which is played behind the pass rush—and the "shell"—which refers to the top of a pass defense, the arrangement of the defensive backs playing behind the underneath coverage.

Creasing the Defense—describes an offense that is able to run the ball with great success against an opponent's defense.

(A. Walsh)

Crossing the Middle—refers to an area of the field where only the boldest of receivers dare to run: the middle of the field. And that's because when their heads are turned to the quarterback to see the ball, they don't see the defensive back coming at them like a heat-seeking missile, and when they extend their arms to catch the ball, they are exposed and get hit hard. Very hard. Shake-the-ball-loose-and-rattle-the-bones hard.

Crowding the Line—describes a defense that is basically "loading the box." It's putting more defenders in the defensive front to stop a running play or a run-based offense, not only in the front but up close to the line of scrimmage.

(Wikipedia)

Cushion—refers to the pre-snap distance or space between a defensive back and a receiver.

Dead Ball—refers to when the ball is not in play.

Defensive Front—refers to that group of defenders opposite the offensive line who can immediately pressure the quarterback or tackle a ballcarrier. It's commonly referred to as "the box." A front will normally consist of seven defenders, but anymore, what with the proliferation of spread offenses, six in the box is a very common sight.

(Thomas Svoboda)

But when defenses want to shut down the run and blitz, they will routinely man-up the wide receivers and "load the box." That means they will add personnel to the front and crowd the line of scrimmage with eight, nine and, sometimes, ten men, making it virtually improbable that the offense can block everyone.

The times you will likely see a defense loading the box are short-yardage situations, like at the goal line, or when they're confronted with a run-first type of offense.

Dime Back—the sixth defensive back in a pass

defense scheme, leaving five defenders to protect against the run. Generally used in obvious passing situations.

Dink and Dunk—refers to a passing attack that focuses on throwing short but quick passes that gain first downs and eat up the clock, like a ball-control offense normally does by running the ball.

Direct Snap—you'd think that this term refers to the snap from the center to the quarterback, but it doesn't. A direct snap is when the ball is snapped directly to the designated ballcarrier and *not* the quarter-back. By eliminating the quarterback from the process, the offense increases the speed of the play and sometimes catches the defense off-guard.

Double Coverage—refers to a pass coverage tactic in which two defensive backs cover one receiver. This often happens to a receiver who's really good, especially in obvious passing situations.

Bracket coverage is double coverage. In fact, it's an ingenious form of double coverage. There are basically two kinds of bracket coverage: in-and-out or high-low. In-and-out is what it's called when two defenders are assigned to one receiver, and the one defender picks up the receiver if he goes inside, while the other picks him if he goes outside. A high-low bracket works much the same way, except one defender has the receiver if he goes deep, while the other has him if he stays short.

Certain pass routes create problems for both man and zone coverages, which in many instances bracket coverage can solve. It's a unique form of double coverage that can eliminate mismatches and still be funda-mentally sound versus the run.

Double Eagle—a unique defensive alignment, often seen used in a 3-4 defense, where the defensive ends (E) "reduce"—which means move inside, towards the ball, and align heads-up on the offensive guards. The linebackers behind them "bump" out to cover the space vacated by the defensive ends, creating a soft spot in the defense known as a "bubble" over the offensive tackles.

Double Move—refers to a receiver tactic in which he runs the stem of his pass route and breaks from it, forcing the defender covering him to react. When the defender does, the receiver then breaks into another route, which fakes out the defender, creating separation.

Down and Distance—see Play Calling.

Drop-Down Safety—refers to the defensive tactic in which a safety, one of the two defensive backs generally assigned to defend the deep end of the field, is repositioned in "the Box" to help shut down an anticipated run play or because the defense intends to blitz.

Edge Defender—coachspeak for the defensive player, generally a defensive end or linebacker, positioned at the end of the offensive line. He's generally the defender who has contain responsibility. (see *Setting the Edge*.)

Empty Set—the term "set" refers to the arrangement of backs in the offensive backfield. Often, you'll hear TV analysts use terms like an "I-set" or a "two-back set" to describe the configuration of the running backs or their number. An "empty set" is exactly what the term implies: there are "zero" running backs. There's only the quarterback, which means there are five wide receivers, as pictured below.

(The Football Brainiacs)

Fair Catch—describes the punt or kick-off return man's decision to not return a kick by waving his arm over his head. He will not be tackled but neither is he allowed to advance the ball. The offense will take possession of the ball where it was caught.

Often, you'll see a player from the punt team run past the return man as he's preparing to catch the ball. That's intentional. The defender is positioning himself to recover the ball in case the return man fumbles it and it rolls or bounces backward.

In the photo below, the punt coverage has formed to contain the return man who is fair catching the ball and to be in position should he fumble the ball backward, behind him. (Photo by *Big House Section 9*)

Field Position—refers to where the ball is spotted on the field—where on the field an offense will initiate a play. Good field position means the offense is going "downhill" on their opponent's side of the 50-yard line. Great field position means they're real close to the end zone. Maybe they're at or beyond the 20-yard line, which is an area of the field known as the "red zone."

Bad field position is the opposite. It means the offense is behind the 50, going "uphill." Really bad field position means they're backed up close to their own end zone, if not up against it.

"Flipping the field" is about turning bad field position for the offense into bad field position for the defense. When the offense punts the ball on fourth down, it's hoping for a long punt so that, when the defense gains possession of the ball, they're stuck deep in their own territory and their offense will start in bad field position. Flipping the field basically means flipping the situation.

The crucial thing about field position is that it affects strategy, the kinds of plays an offense calls when it's "coming out" of its end of the field versus the plays it would call going into its opponent's end zone.

The same is true with the defense. When their opponent is in bad field position, they might take more risks to create a turnover or a tackle for a loss that would put the offense "behind the chains"—which refers to a situation where they have to gain some significant yardage to earn a first down. This, too, would impact what plays the offense would use and the tactics the defense would employ to stop it.

Down-and-distance and field position are the two factors that most influence the tactics being used on the field. While high-reward tactics make the game exciting and unpredictable, they also come with high risks. If the high-reward tactics work, the coach is bold and brilliant. If not, he's not.

Field Side (Wideside)—see *Boundary (Shortside)*.

Fire Zone—see *Zone Blitz*.

First and Goal—describes the situation where the offense, after earning a first down, is so close to the end zone that there's not enough yardage left to earn another. The only thing left to do is score in the four downs awarded them.

First Down—refers to the first play in a series of four plays granted the offense to gain the necessary yardage, usually ten yards, to be awarded another first down, or series of four plays. A "down" is basically nothing more than a "play." As long as the offense is gaining "first downs," it can retain possession of the ball. When it doesn't, it has to surrender possession of the ball by punting it on fourth down.

Flea-flicker—is a trick play, but it's a special kind of trick play. It starts with the quarterback handing the ball off to a running back, which causes the defense to attack because they're thinking it's a run play. This in turn allows a receiver to break clear of the deep coverage and attack the middle.

Just as the running back appears to reach the line of scrimmage, he turns and laterals the ball back to the quarterback, who has retreated into the backfield to give himself some cushion from the rush. The quarterback then throws to the open receiver, as the defense can't change direction fast enough to defend against the pass.

The flea-flicker is not a modern creation. It was developed by Bob Zuppke, the head coach at the University of Illinois, who revealed in a 1951 letter that he had used the play as far back as 1910 at Oak Park High School. Zuppke explained that the play's unique backfield action was intended to remind spectators of the "... quick flicking action of a dog getting rid of fleas."

Maybe in 1911, but not now.

FOOTBALL FOR MOMS AND SWEETHEARTS

(Larry Brown Sports)

Flipping the Field—see *Field Position*.

Force—see the section *Defending the Run*.

Front Seven—refers to the seven defensive players—the defensive linemen and linebackers—who are arrayed in what is often called "the box," but is technically known as the defensive front.

Gap—is the space between the offensive linemen, while a "line split" is the distance. Gaps are "soft spots" in a defense and are routinely attacked by running plays. For identification purposes, they are lettered from the inside out as illustrated below. Every time a player is added to the end of the line, another gap is created.

(LOC Photography)

Goal-Line Stand—describes when the defense has reared up and stuffed the offense at the goal line and prevented it from scoring.

Half the Distance to the Goal Line—penalties assessed near a team's end zone are cut in half because there's often not enough yardage from where the ball is spotted, or where the violation occurred, to the goal line to walk off the yardage lost for a particular offense.

Hail Mary—refers to the desperation long pass thrown near the closing seconds of a game to win the game or, in the case of the closing seconds of the first half, to gain the lead or simply score.

The idea is to throw the ball deep and high so that receivers can cluster in the area where it is descending and either leap high into the air and catch the ball or catch the ball when it's tipped by a defender. That's why you'll see receivers on the ground, around the players leaping into the air, so they're in position to catch a tipped ball.

Hail Mary

Arc of leather, dizzy brown,
Spinning tightly, round and round,
Curving earthward, downward bound,
To upstretched hand, or plush green ground.
Eyes turned upward and spellbound,
Await the outcome without a sound.

Copyright©1996 - All Rights Reserved.

Hang Time—refers to the length of time a punt hangs in the air, which is actually its height. The longer—or higher—the better, as that allows the punt coverage team to get to the return man and tackle him before he can make a move upfield.

Hard Count—is an attempt to draw the defense offsides by calling a signal more loudly than the others. The risk, however, is that the hard count can also make an offensive lineman false start.

Hat in the Crack—see the slice *"Hat in the Crack."*

"I" Formation—an offensive formation and run-based offensive sys-tem devised by Tom Nugent in the early '50s at VMI. The "I"—which has endured the test of time—is still a popular offensive system at all levels of competition, and is a mainstay in the pros.

The "I" got its name from how the running backs are lined up in a straight line behind the quarterback which, when viewed from above, looks like the letter "i."

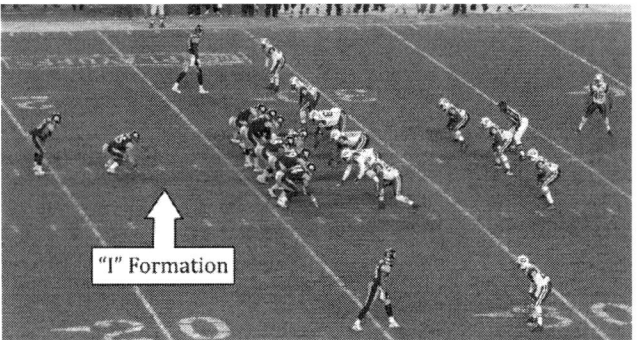

"I" Formation
(Wikipedia)

The "I" is a formidable offense, as it can run with power because of the lead blocker in front of the I-back (or tailback), and if needed, it can release 3-4 receivers into pass routes.

Icing the Kicker—is about the defense getting into the kicker's head just before he's about to kick a field goal—especially a game-winning field goal. What the coach does is wait until the last possible second before the kicker engages the ball and calls a time out. The idea—the hope—is that during the time out, the kicker overthinks the situation and his nerves get to him so that when does kick the ball, he misses.

Inside (Outside, Off-tackle)—there are inside and outside running plays, and in between the two is a little area called "off-tackle." Inside running plays attack between the offensive tackles. Outside running plays, on the other hand, attack a defense's perimeter. They run at or outside the defense's end man on the line, the guy coaches routinely refer to as an edge defender.

(Robert Welch)

Off-tackle, meanwhile, is the area over the offensive tackles. Its width will vary with the split of the end man on the defensive line—and area often called the "edge." The area widens farther if the offense positions a tight end outside the offensive tackle.

Inside-Out Pursuit—refers to the defensive players coming from the defensive front who are pursuing a run play that is attacking outside and being channeled back inside, towards them, by the "force" defender to that side of the field.

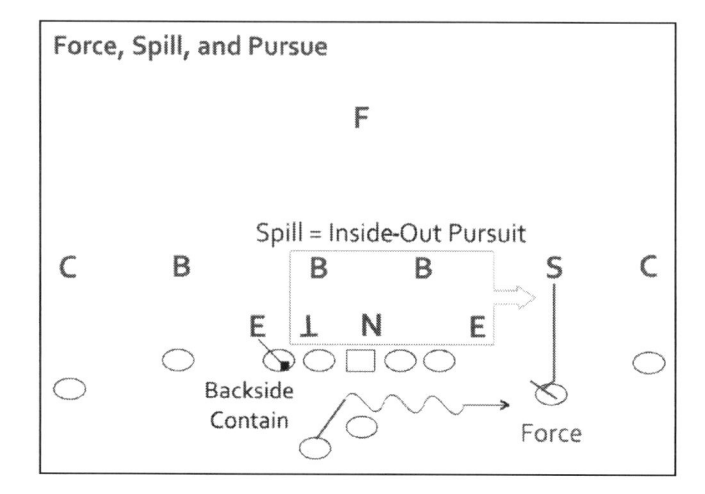

Force, Spill, and Pursue

Interception—refers to a forward pass that has been caught by a defensive player rather than the offensive receiver for whom it was intended. The theft results in a change of possession. The ball now belongs to the defensive team.

Keeping a Clean Pocket—is an expression referring to the pass protection—the pass blocking of the offensive line. The goal of all pass blocking is to keep the quarterback upright and his uniform "clean" by not letting him get tackled to the ground.

(MG Thomson)

Leveraging the Offense—describes what a defense has done when it "contains" an offense by preventing it from running outside, in a defense's perimeter where it is weakest. (See *Defending the Run*.)

Line of Scrimmage—is an imaginary line that crosses the field where the ball is spotted. Neither the offensive or defensive players can cross the line of scrimmage until the football is snapped and the play started. (See *Neutral Zone*.)

What is not common knowledge is that there are actually two lines of scrimmage, one each at either tip of the ball. One for the offense, and one for the defense. In between the two is the neutral zone, which no can enter except the center, and only him because he has to handle the ball to snap it.

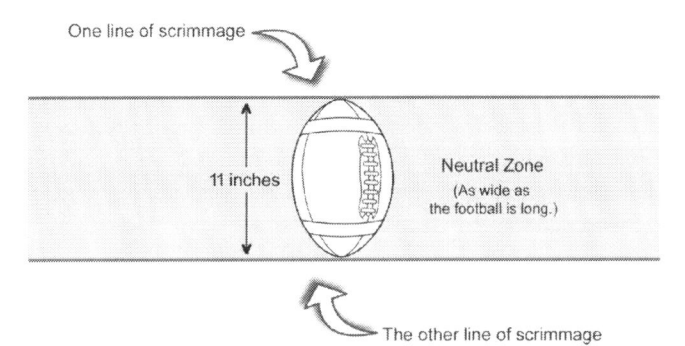

Line Splits—is the distance between offensive linemen, while gaps are the spaces. Line splits will vary in width, depending upon what the offense is seeking to achieve.

> **Standard Line Splits** – compare the distance between the offensive line in the dark uniforms to that seen in the offensive lines in the photos that follow of tight and wide line splits.

(Wikipedia)

Tight splits, where the offensive linemen are aligned foot to foot, generally means the offense is preparing to bulldoze the defense and it doesn't want any "leakage"—meaning a defender penetrating into the backfield through a gap.

You'll often see tight line splits in short-yardage situations where the offense needs a yard or two to gain a first down or in goal-line situations like that pictured below.

Tight Line Splits

(Wikipedia)

Wide splits, used by many uptempo, no-huddle teams, create wide running lanes in a defense for a running back to exploit, and more importantly, they stretch a defense's edge defenders farther out from the quarterback, giving him more time to throw the ball.

Wide Line Splits

(Syracuse Fans)

Offensive linemen routinely adjust their splits to better perform their blocking assignments, either to widen a defender or to shorten the distance to him, thus increasing the speed of the block.

Loading the Box—refers to the defensive tactic of inserting defensive backs into the defensive front—what is called "the box"—in anticipation of a pass play to blitz and sack the quarterback or versus a run play to shut down the ballcarrier. You'll see it done routinely in short-yardage situations when an offense needs four yards or less for a first down or at the goal line, where the offense is threatening to score.

Looking into the Backfield—is bad news for the defense playing man-to-man coverage when one of its defensive backs is "looking into the offensive backfield" to see what the play is instead of focusing on his assigned receiver, which is what he's supposed to do in man coverage. The mistake can be costly, as the receiver can get past him and into the open field.

Man-to-Man—see *Defending the Pass*.

Mike, Will, and Sam—see the Slice under the *Linebacker* section.

Move the Pile—describes the running back who is so strong and powerful that he moves forward a pile of tacklers trying to bring him down. Most often seen at the goal line or in short-yardage situations, where the energy levels are the highest.

(YouTube)

Naked Boot (Naked)—see *Bootleg*.

Neutral Zone—the neutral zone is the no man's land between the opposing teams created by the football when it is spotted ready for play. What it does is divide the field into an offensive and defensive side and it is as wide as a football is long: 11 inches.

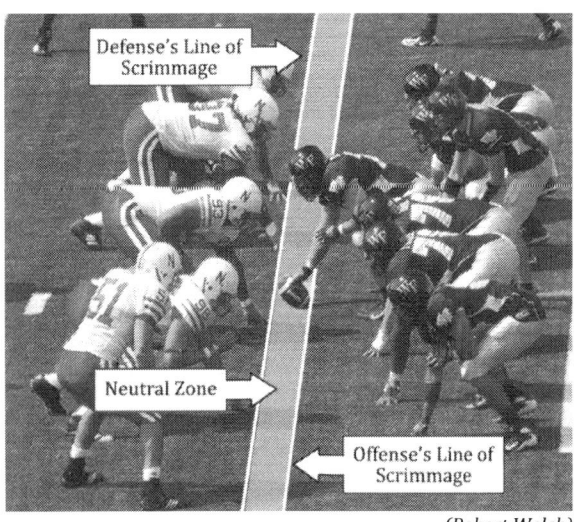

(Robert Welch)

The neutral zone also creates two imaginary lines of scrimmage, with each line intersecting a tip of the football and extending to the sideline: one line for the defense and one for the offense.

Other than the center, no one can be in the neutral zone, and only him because he has to grip the ball to snap it. Anyone else lining up in the neutral zone is a violation and will result in a penalty, costing the offending team five yards.

Nickle Back—refers to the fifth defensive back in a pass defense. Seen a lot versus spread teams who release four or five receivers into pass routes.

No-Huddle—describes an offensive system in which the offense doesn't huddle and tries to start a play in 15 seconds or less. The faster, the better. Uptempo is the term often used to describe the no-huddle scheme.

Off-setting Penalties—refers to offenses committed by both teams in the same play that cancel each other out.

Off-Tackle—see *Inside, Outside, Off-Tackle*.

On an Island—describes a cornerback's situation when he is covering an offense's widest and best receiver, without any help from the deep safeties. They are often by themselves or "on an island" in trying to defend a stud pass catcher.

Outside—see *Inside, Outside, Off-Tackle*.

Over (Under)—refers to special alignments peculiar to the 4-3 defense. The 4-3 defense was already around when Jimmy Johnson and the Miami Hurricane morphed into the 4-3 Over scheme to combat the Wishbone offenses of the 80's—particularly that of the Oklahoma Sooners.

Once coaches saw the success the Hurricane had with the Over variation, the scheme became wildly popular. The "Over" alignment puts the defensive tackle, the defender positioned as a "3" technique on the strong side—the side with the most blockers—while the "Under" alignment places him on the weakside.

The linemen in a 4-3 only have one gap to defend, so

their objective is not to read any blocks, but to penetrate the backfield. As might be expected, the defensive linemen are stunting quite a bit to keep the offensive line guessing. There are three bubbles in the Over, and two in the Under.

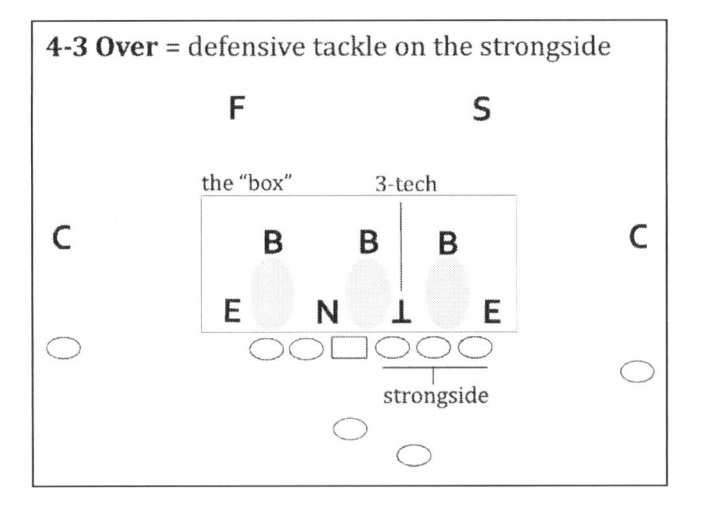

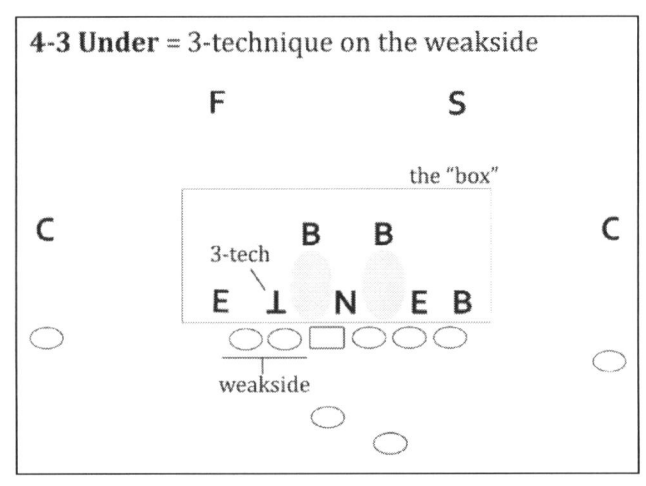

4-3 Over = defensive tackle on the strongside

4-3 Under = 3-technique on the weakside

Play-Action Pass—refers to a pass play that starts out looking like a run play. The run fake either freezes the defense momentarily or causes the linebackers to attack the line of scrimmage, which opens up the field behind them to an attack from a pass.

The key, however, is that the offense must be having some success running the ball for the run fake to work; otherwise, the defense won't react to the fake. Also called a "run fake" by some TV commentators.

Playside—see *Backside (Playside)*.

Pick—is jargon for a forward pass that's been intercepted by a defensive player.

Pick Play—is a pass play in which, by design, a receiver, or receivers, actually interfere with defenders to impede or redirect them so that another receiver can break into the open grass created and catch a pass. The interference—called a "rub" or "natural rub" by coaches— is made to look like incidental contact, which is allowed. Pick plays are routinely performed near the end zone, where there isn't much-to-no room to throw deep. It works best against man-to-man defenses.

Pick Six—refers to a pass interception that has resulted in a touchdown which equals six points.

Pocket—is jargon for the way the offensive line looks when it sets up pass protection for the quarterback. It will often look like a "pocket" or a "cup" if the quarterback has retreated after the snap and set up directly behind the center.

(LOC Photography)

Pocket Passer—describes the quarterback who stands tall in the "pocket" and surveys the field before throwing to an open receiver. The other designation is "dual-threat," which refers to the quarterback who can "extend a play" because of scrambling ability.

Pooch Kick—is a high, short kick to a designated area of the field so the coverage team can swarm and contain the ballcarrier quickly, thus reducing any chance of a long return.

Press Coverage—describes pass coverage that is up close and personal, meaning in the face of the receiver. The idea is to prevent what is called a free release from the line by a receiver by physically jamming him and attempting to reroute him, meaning force him to change his assignment.

(Steve Cheng)

Many pass routes are timed routes. These are routes whose length and time to execute is matched to the time it takes a quarterback to set up and throw the ball. Press coverage—what is also called "bump-and-run" coverage—seeks to disrupt that timing, thus giving the defensive line and anyone blitzing the quarterback a chance to sack him before he can throw the ball.

Prevent Defense—sometimes prevent nothing. At the end of a game in which the defense is leading, they back up deep to prevent the offense from completing any long passes or runs that could result in a score, while rushing three or four players to force a throw or run.

The idea is to keep everything—most particularly the player with the ball—in front of them and to not let him get out of bounds, which stops the clock. The problem is that the defense gives up so much open grass for the offense to attack that, often, the offense is able to march toward the end zone and place themselves in a better position to complete a long pass—like a Hail Mary—and score.

Pursuit—see the section Defending the Run.

Quarterback Sneak—is quite possibly football's easiest play, especially in short-yardage situations. The strategy is simple: the quarterback plunges head first into the line, slipping through a crease created by the offensive line that is pile driving the defense in front of him. It's so simple that most teams never practice it.

But it wasn't until 1938, when the quarterback started to align under center that the "sneak"—with its quick snap and the sudden, powerful surge of the offensive line—truly caught defenses by surprise.

Football's Coldest Game

Football's coldest game ever was won on a quarterback sneak. Christened "The Ice Bowl" by the media, the 1967 NFL Championship game was played in Green Bay, Wisconsin where the average temperature at game time was a -26° C and the wind chill factor measured at -44° C.

It was so cold that, during warm-ups, the woodwind instruments of the Wisconsin-Whitewater band froze and would not play, while the mouthpieces of the brass instruments stuck to the band members' lips. During the game, an elderly Green Bay fan died from exposure.

But when it counted most was when the game was coldest. With 16 seconds left in the game and the ball at the Dallas two-foot line, Green Bay called a time out. Bart Starr, the Packer quarterback, went to the sideline to confer with legendary head coach Vince Lombardi. Two attempts at pounding the ball in from the one-yard line had failed. The turf was frozen, yet Starr asked right guard Jerry Kramer if he could get enough traction to run a wedge play.

The stoic Kramer said yes.

Everyone—particularly the Dallas Cowboys—was thinking the Packers would call a roll-out pass play. It made perfect sense given the circumstances. The frozen ground had weakened Green Bay's pass protection and allowed Dallas to sack Starr eight times, so a roll-out pass would remove Starr from the rush.

But more importantly, because Green Bay had no time-outs to stop the clock if a run play failed, the roll-out pass would stop the clock if it were incomplete. Green Bay would have time to kick a field goal and send the game into overtime.

FOOTBALL FOR MOMS AND SWEETHEARTS

But Starr had a different idea.

(pckerville.blogspot)

Rather than hand the ball off to a running back who might slip and fall, Starr considered his proximity at quarterback to the end zone, telling Lombardi that if the offensive linemen could get their feet dug in, he was close enough "... to shuffle my feet and lunge in." Lombardi thought about it for a second then agreed. "Run it," he said without hesitation, "and let's get the hell out of here."

In the huddle, Starr called, "Brown Right 31 Wedge." The play was designed for the fullback to run the ball, but Starr told no one he was keeping it. Kramer and center Ken Bowman performed a perfect double-team block on Dallas' All-Pro defensive tackle, Jethro Pugh, and much to the surprise of everyone in the stadium, Starr plunged head first into the end zone for a 20-17 lead.

(Keyword Suggest)

Don Chandler kicked the extra point, and after the kick-off, Dallas threw two incomplete passes to finish the game. It was altogether fitting, if not divinely scripted, that Green Bay should win football's coldest game, 21-17, using its simplest play—the one not even diagrammed in most playbooks.

Red Zone—coachspeak for that area of the field starting at an opponent's 20-yard line and extending to the goal line. Here offensive and defensive strategy changes dramatically because the field has shrunken. There are no deep passes, so there's less space or "open grass" to attack and defend.

It's here where you'll see a lot of pick plays where the offense is anticipating man coverage, so they'll call plays in which a receiver(s) actually interferes with a defender's attempts to cover the designated pass catcher. The key is that the interference look incidental, what coaches call a "natural rub," so that the officials don't penalize the offense for pass interference.

Rolled Coverage—describes a pass coverage strategy in which the defense shows one scheme before the snap then "rolls" into something else afterward. As with most things a defense does before the snap, the idea is to disguise its intentions.

RPO—is an acronym for "Run-Pass Option." It's a really nifty offensive play that can attack a defense three different ways. Two of them are run plays, and the third is a pass play. The key is how the defense reacts.

In the first phase of the play, the quarterback puts the ball in the running back's grasp while reading the reaction of a designated defender. If the defender looks to attack the running back, the quarterback pulls the ball and runs to the outside of the formation, where he initiates the RPO's second phase.

Now in the perimeter, the quarterback reads the reaction of another designated defender: the one defending the play's primary receiver who has faked a block on the defender and streaked past him. If the defender "flips his hips" and covers the receiver, the quarterback runs the ball. If, however, the defender releases the receiver to pursue the quarterback the quarterback throws the ball to what is often, a wide-open receiver.

Rub Play—see *Pick Play*.

Run-Action—see *Play-Action Pass*.

Run Out the Clock—refers to the offensive strategy of running the ball to preserve the lead near the end of a game. The idea is to "run" out the clock, because the clock doesn't stop after a run play but does after an incomplete pass. Run plays eat time and force the defense to call time outs, to preserve time for the their offense.

Sack—describes when a quarterback has been tackled behind the line of scrimmage for lost yardage.

Scrambling—is jargon for when a quarterback runs around in the backfield to avoid being sacked while looking for an open receiver or deciding to run with the ball.

Screen Pass—is a quarterback's best friend and definitely an aid to an offensive line facing an aggressive pass rush. The play, which in various forms can be found in every offensive coordinator's playbook, is designed to exploit a defense that's too eager to sack a quarterback. Be looking for it when, after setting up to throw, the quarterback starts to retreat even more, as if to avoid the rush of the defensive line and any blitzers. Chances are that he's doing it intentionally.

The idea is to draw the defenders towards him, to get them separated from the offensive linemen who have feigned pass blocking and allowed the defense to rush past them. In the space created between the two, a running back has set up to receive a pass from the quarterback who lofts the ball over the heads of the defenders attacking him. The running back then alerts the offensive linemen, who are scanning the field for a defender to block, that he has the ball, and all charge forward.

A screen play is one of the few times an offensive lineman can cross the line of scrimmage (LOS) during a pass play because the pass is behind the LOS. The defensive linemen and anyone blitzing take themselves out of the play in their zeal to get to the quarterback and sack him.

The basic screen is a middle screen to a running back. It is performed in the middle of the offensive formation like that described above. It can be directed at a running back or a tight end. But screens aren't limited to the middle of the offensive formation—only to behind the line of scrimmage, and anywhere there.

Setting the Edge—is coachspeak for when the edge defender—the defensive player at either end of the line—prevents the ballcarrier from getting outside where the defense is weakest. He does that by containing him in the backfield, so that the pursuit coming from the defensive front can catch him or by "spilling" him—which is another way to contain him—by forcing him to run toward the sideline and not cross the line of scrimmage, thus not gain any yardage. Setting the edge is critical to a defense's efforts to stop the run.

> In the photo below, the defensive end (#90) has "set the edge" by forcing the ballcarrier back into the pursuit coming from the linebacker (#50).

(Guy Herbert)

Shortside—see Boundary.

Shovel Pass—is a nifty little pass play thrown behind the line of scrimmage to an eligible receiver that looks like an illegal forward lateral. A lateral has to be thrown backward and underhanded. But the shovel pass doesn't because it's thrown overhanded, making it a legal forward pass. It's sort of like a screen in that it's often used to counter an aggressive pass rush.

(Lizard Pad)

FOOTBALL FOR MOMS AND SWEETHEARTS

The key difference is that the offensive line channels the rush to the outside, which opens up a lane in the middle of the formation that the receiver curls into as he catches the pass. And the neat thing about the shovel is that, if the receiver drops the ball, it's not a fumble but an incomplete pass.

Also known as the Utah Pass where it was first introduced to football, the shovel pass is often incurrectly referred to as the "shuffle pass."

Sky Coverage—describes who plays deep in a three-deep zone pass defense, what is routinely called "Cover 3." In "sky" coverage, the two cornerbacks and a safety cover the deep zones. While it's counterpart, "cloud" coverage has one cornerback and two safeties handle the deep part of the field. The terms also describe who has "force" responsibility to one side of the field. In "sky" it's a safety and in "cloud," it's a cornerback.

Sluggo—is a popular pass route using a double move by a receiver to defeat man-to-man coverage. To influence the defensive back covering him, away from the "go" route, which is the money route, the receiver first runs a "slant," which draws him inside, clearing the space outside. Then, once the defender has bit on the slant, the receiver breaks to the "go" route, which separates him from the defensive back and attacks the deep end of the field.

It's a sweet route!

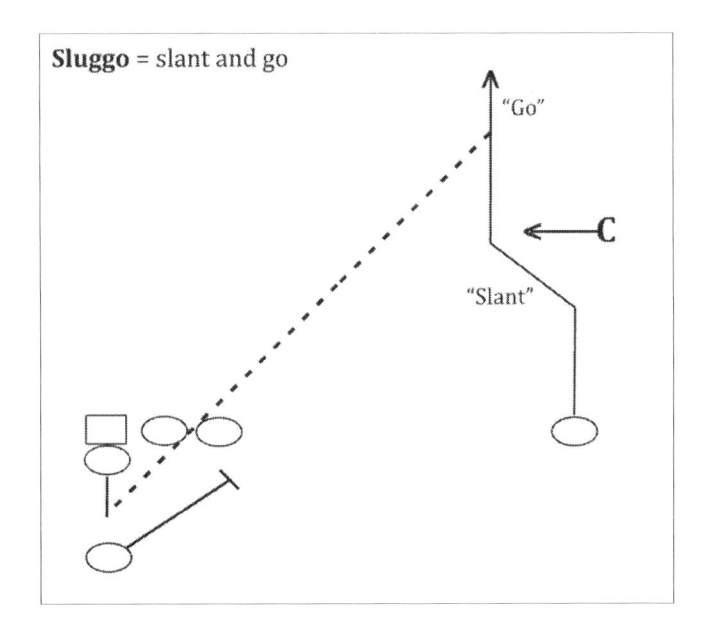

Sluggo = slant and go

Soft Coverage—describes the pre-snap alignment of a defensive back who has given the receiver he's covering a lot of "cushion"—meaning space. The idea is to not allow the receiver to get deep and to force the quarterback to throw short to him, thus keeping the play in front of the defensive back.

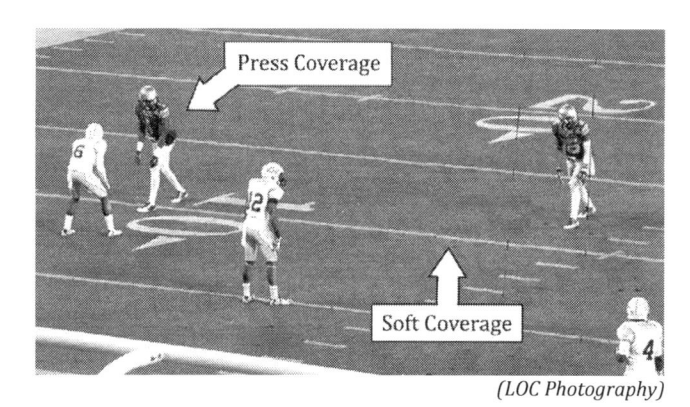

(LOC Photography)

Squeeze—refers to the defensive tactic of preventing a ballcarrier who is attacking "outside" from gaining yardage by "squeezing" him into the sideline, that is, forcing him to run parallel to the line of scrimmage and into the sideline. In football terms, the ballcarrier is forced to run east to west, which gains no yardage. Rather than north to south, which does.

Squib Kick—is like the "pooch kick" in that the intent is to disrupt the blocking and minimize the return. The squib kick, however, is kicked hard and close to the ground so that the ball shoots through the front line of the return team and tumbles, making it difficult to handle. Bill Walsh of Super Bowl and San Francisco 49er fame reportedly saw the kick used in a high school game and credits the coach, Mike Squib, with its development.

Staying Ahead of the Chains—is coachspeak for an offense gaining positive yardage on first down so that, on 2nd and 3rd down, the guy calling the plays—the offensive coordinator—can choose from a variety of plays in the playbook to earn the first down. Conversely, losing yardage on first down, either because of a penalty or a tackle for a loss, like a sack, will limit what he can call on 2nd and 3rd down, which is advantage for the defense. The situation is also referred to as "staying on schedule."

Stemming—refers to a shift of the defensive linemen just before the ball is snapped. The sudden change in positions can confuse the offensive line's blocking scheme, so that some defender breaks free into the offensive backfield and tackles the ball-carrier or the quarterback for a loss.

Strongside (Weakside)—refers to the side of an offensive formation that has the most blockers to execute a run play. The weakside, then, is the side with the least. Defenses align their personnel according to where the strongside of an offensive formation is, to match strength with strength.

Stunt—see *Stunting and Blitzing*.

Sugar in the A Gaps—is coachspeak for when the defense aligns a linebacker in each A gap—the space between the center and the guards on either side. The idea is to intimidate the offensive line and force it to change its blocking scheme to handle the blitz they think is coming. Except that, after the snap, the linebackers often drop into pass coverage.

(The Rookie Scouting Report)

Take the Top Off a Defense—refers to the offense practice of attacking defenses with receivers who have the speed to stretch the pass coverage vertically, specifically the safeties who are routinely positioned deepest in the defense. This strategy, if successful, opens the field underneath to short or intermediate passes, as well as opening up the run game.

Turnover—refers to a fumble or interception in which the offense has lost possession of the ball to the defense.

Unbalanced Line—describes the offensive line that either has two offensive tackles positioned on the same side of the line or four or more offensive linemen positioned to one side, creating a heavy or jumbo formation. The intent is throw off the defense as to how to match up to the odd formation and, at the same time, add more power the side of the formation the offense looks to be attacking.

Utah Pass—see *Shovel Pass*.

Victory Formation— before the Victory formation—which offers a lot of protection against a turnover—was seen in football, teams would run quarterback sneaks to "kill the clock" and preserve a victory.

But Herm Edwards changed all of that when, on November 19, 1978, he recovered a fumbled hand-off and ran it back for a game-winning touchdown in what has been called the "Miracle of the Meadowlands." Within a week, the Eagles and Giants came up with better ideas, which evolved into the "victory" formation pictured below. Now everybody uses it.

(Philadelphia.com)

Waggle—is a term that comes to us from an old University of Delaware playbook. It refers to a "bootleg" play that attacks a defense's weakside and has the two offensive guards—the guys on either side of the center—provide protection for the quarterback. (See *Bootleg*.)

Weakside—see *Strongside*.

Wedge Blocking—is pure power. Everyone on the offensive line steps to the man inside of the them and seals the gap between them while staying low and driving forward. Like the blade on a snow plow, the offensive line pushes the defense off the line and, through sheer mass and momentum, overpowers the defenders. It's a great way to gain a few yards when needed, so look for it in goal line situations.

Wideside—see *Boundary (Shortside)*.

Wildcat—is an offensive package often seen in college football and sometimes in the pros that has the quarterback line up as a wide receiver, and a wide receiver—or running back—takes a direct snap from the center. The formation itself will often feature an unbalanced line and have a player crossing in motion from one side to the other prior to the snap. Basically, it's a trick play designed to keep a defense guessing because its unconventional.

The Wildcat itself is a spin off from Pop Warner's Single Wing offense that dominated offensive thinking back in the '20s until the advent of the T-Formation. Invented by Billy Ford and Ryan Wilson, it was originally called the "Dual" formation. But in the hands of the Kansas State Wildcats coaching staff, for whom the concept was named, the Wildcat has become a common feature in college football.

Zone Coverage—see *Defending the Pass*.

Zone Blitz—a blitz in which a zone defense, instead of the customary man to man, is being run behind it and a defensive lineman has dropped into one of the zones near the line of scrimmage. Usually, quarterbacks see a man-to-man defense behind a blitz and don't expect a defensive lineman to pop up in coverage. It's the defensive form of trickeration. More commonly known as a "Zone Dog" or a "Fire Zone."

Zone Dog—see *Zone Blitz*.

A BLAST FROM THE PAST

The President Who Saved Football

(History Things)

Concussions weren't a pressing issue in the early days of football. Dying was. So, after 18 players had been killed and 159 critically injured playing the game in 1905, President Theodore Roosevelt—no stranger himself to rugged play—gave the ruling powers of football a choice: change the game or see it abolished by Executive Order.

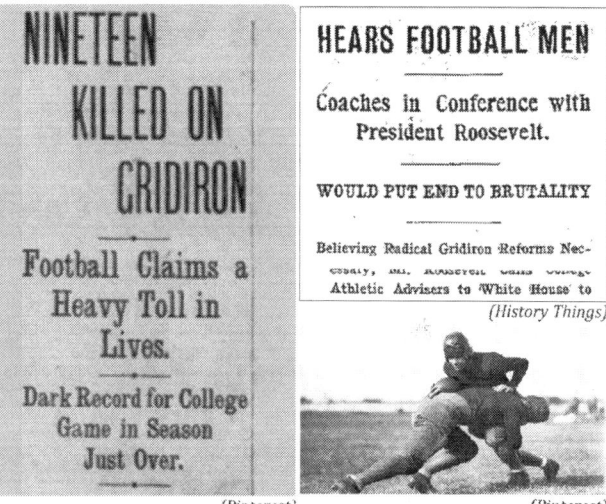

(Wikipedia)

NINETEEN KILLED ON GRIDIRON

Football Claims a Heavy Toll in Lives.

Dark Record for College Game in Season Just Over.

(Pinterest)

HEARS FOOTBALL MEN

Coaches in Conference with President Roosevelt.

WOULD PUT END TO BRUTALITY

Believing Radical Gridiron Reforms Necessary, Mr. Roosevelt Calls College Athletic Advisers to White House to

(History Things)

(Pinterest)

As much as he loved the toughness that football ingrained in America's youth, Roosevelt—and much of eastern society—had wearied of its savagery. It was, by numerous descriptions, no better than brawling, not only because of the numerous fist fights that routinely erupted at games, but mostly because of an offensive strategy called "mass-momentum plays."

The concept of massing players into tightly woven formations to increase their power at the point of attack began in 1884 during a game between Princeton and Penn.

In an attempt to break a 0-0 deadlock, Princeton quarterback Richard Hodge devised a play in which the "rush line"—an early version of an offensive line—jumped into a wedge or V-shaped formation at the snap of the ball and plowed forward like a tank through the Penn defense with the ballcarrier safely tucked in behind. The men from Penn had no answer for the trick formation and were routed 31-0.

The "V-trick," as it would later be called, was the first of many innovative formations to follow that relied

FOOTBALL FOR MOMS AND SWEETHEARTS

on massing players together and slamming them into defenses like some ancient Greek phalanx. The most lethal of these formations was Harvard's infamous Flying Wedge.

V-Trick

(Tumblr)

The brainchild of a Boston lawyer and avid chess player who never played football, the Flying Wedge took advantage of the rule that permitted offenses to mass some distance from the spot of the ball and advance towards it at a run, gaining speed and power just as the ball is snapped. That allowed them to plunge headlong into the thin ranks of an opposing defense and bulldoze through them.

(Wikipedia)

The Flying Wedge divided the offense into two groups of five men each at opposite sidelines, about 20 yards from the spot of the ball. When signaled, and before the ball was snapped, each unit sprinted at full speed toward the center of the field where it formed a "massive human arrow" (pictured below), at which point the ball was pitched back to the halfback in the rear. Meanwhile, restricted by the rules, the defense would hold their positions, waiting for the onslaught.

When confronted with this form of attack, a defense had two choices: stand their ground or throw themselves into the path of the wedge. In either case, the effects of Lorin Deland's creation, designed on a chessboard, were devastating. The impacts were horrific, if not deadly.

Lorin Deland

Football's popularity suffered for its violence and also because the game's main attraction—the ballcarrier—was often obscured by the roiling mass of bodies resulting from the constant collisions.

Part of the problem was that mass-momentum formations were in vogue long before anyone thought of using protective equipment like helmets, facemasks, and shoulders pads. In their absence, the number of serious injuries and deaths in the game increased dramatically; so much so that newspapers routinely reported them along with a game's statistics.

The other part of the problem was the rules that allowed offenses to go in motion prior to the snap. In response to public pressure, football effectively outlawed the Flying Wedge and other mass-momentum formations like it when they changed the rules and restricted the number of men to three who could go in motion before the snap.

The new rules, however, permitted teams to pull linemen into the backfield, which allowed for a running start. Also, teams could send running backs in motion before the snap. The effect was not entirely unlike the Flying Wedge, as both tactics still allowed an offense to mass against a defense at the point of attack.

The carnage continued. Players were often strewn across the field in broken heaps, and slugfests still erupted regularly. Many players died. It was then, in 1906, that Roosevelt, more from a desire to save the game than to see it disbanded, intervened and delivered his ultimatum.

FOOTBALL FOR MOMS AND SWEETHEARTS

This time football responded by introducing helmets and knee pads to the game. It also legalized the forward pass, whose true potential as an offensive weapon wasn't fully realized until 1913.

(iHave.net)

But the rule that resulted in the creation of an offensive line and reduced the level of violence in the game came in 1910. It mandated that seven offensive players must be on the line of scrimmage prior to the ball being snapped. They could not move until the ball was snapped.

Carlisle Indians

(Wikipedia)

With this new rule, football completely eliminated mass-momentum formations. And with the advent of the forward pass, it changed how football would be played. The two players on either side of the line would become eligible receivers, leaving five men to play along the interior. One had to snap the ball and the other four became "pushers" or blockers.

These five positions, like every other position, became specialized. They became the offensive line. The only thing that has changed about the offensive line since 1910 is the size, skill, and strength of modern "pushers."

In almost all cases, they are not eligible to catch a pass. And they cannot go in motion. They are why most offensive formations—be it a spread or something heavy like an "I"—will look like that pictured above: five guys up front with the quarterback and the running back(s) behind and the receivers to the side.

As a direct result of Theodore Roosevelt's threat to abolish football, we now have protective equipment, the forward pass, and an offensive line. And, believe it or not, a lot less violence.

Modern "pushers"

(YouTube)

ADDENDUM ONE

Football's Six Basic Pass Defenses

All pass defense starts with the pass rush. In most cases, that consists of four defensive linemen, which leaves seven defenders to cover the five eligible receivers the offense can release into a pass pattern. They are routinely deployed into three types of pass defenses: zone, man, or a combination of zone-man schemes called "combos."

Zone defenses have defenders read the quarterback and protect specific areas of the field. Man defenses, on the other hand, have defenders read an assigned receiver and cover him wherever he goes. Combo defenses, as was described previously, have some defenders playing zone and others playing man to man.

The variety and complexity of coverage schemes is limited only by the speed and skill of the defenders and the imagination of the defensive coordinator. Basically, though, there are six coverage schemes that can be tweaked each week to match up to an

FOOTBALL FOR MOMS AND SWEETHEARTS

opponent's strengths or from which everything else evolves. You can easily identify them, as there are features to each that make them unique and recognizable.

When you look at a defense, start your "read" at the top, where the two safeties are routinely positioned. Their number—be it one, two, or zero—will begin to unravel what the defense's intentions are.

Cover 0

The easiest of the six schemes to identify is the first: Cover 0. What coaches call "zero man." It's easy to identify because there's no one positioned deep, hence the term "zero." But it also means that there's zero help for the defenders underneath who are "manned up" on each receiver. If a receivers breaks free from his defender, he's gone to the house.

Meanwhile, the pass defenders underneath are aligned up close and personal to the receivers in what is called "press" coverage. They're focused entirely on their assigned receiver because they want to impede his "free release" from the line and disrupt the timing of his pass route. They want to "reroute" him and give the pass rush time to sack the quarterback.

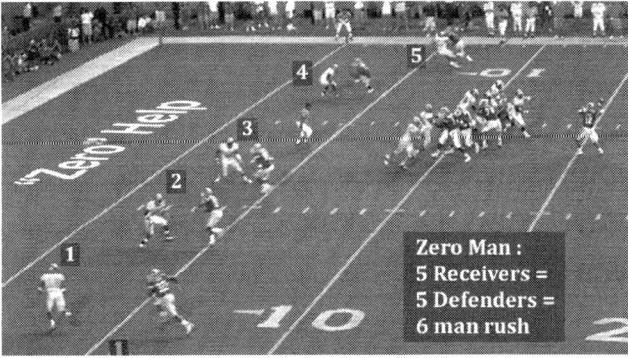

Zero Man:
5 Receivers =
5 Defenders =
6 man rush

(BJ Smith)

This scheme is great versus the run because the box is loaded. But it's also high risk versus the pass because, as mentioned before, there's no "deep" help. A mistake like a misstep, a stumble, or a misread by a defender who is singled up on a receiver can result in a quick touchdown by the offense.

But it can also be high reward if the receivers are thwarted, because defenses that call up a "zero man" scheme are planning to blitz. Which means they will likely outnumber the blockers and have a good chance to get to the quarterback before he can throw to an open receiver.

Remember, in Cover 0, there's no one playing centerfield—to borrow a baseball term—and the defenders are aligned tight to the offense, with the pass defenders focused on their receiver.

Zero Man:
5 Receivers =
5 Defenders =
6 man rush

(Football Concepts)

Cover 1

The next coverage scheme that you can easily spot is Cover 1. What coaches call "man free." It's easy to spot because there's only one safety positioned in the deep middle. That's generally the free safety who, in this alignment, is commonly referred to as the "single-high safety" and, because he's playing zone, he's "free" to help deep whoever needs it.

The other safety, meanwhile, is probably in "the box," looking to blitz. While the "man" reference, like in "zero man," means that the other underneath defenders are manned up, one on one with a receiver.

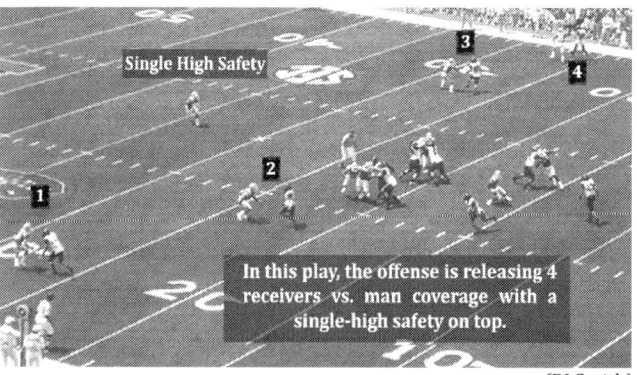

Single High Safety

In this play, the offense is releasing 4 receivers vs. man coverage with a single-high safety on top.

(BJ Smith)

If those defenders are in a "press' alignment, they're wanting to reroute the receiver and give the pass rush time to get to the quarterback.

But if the cornerbacks—the defenders positioned

opposite the offense's widest receivers—are playing "off"—that is, giving their receiver some "cushion"—then there's a good chance they may "bail" and drop back into a Cover 3 defense, which I discuss below. You'll know if they're changing to this coverage because, just before the ball is snapped, the cornerbacks will "bail" or sprint backward into deep zone coverage.

This scheme is not as high risk as zero-man because of the single-high safety, who can help a defender whose receiver breaks free and goes deep. What occurs then is that the receiver gets "double coverage" from the defender manned up on him and the single-high safety. Cover 1 is often used to give an offense a false read because, after the ball is snapped, it can quickly change into Cover 3 or some other coverage.

So, when you see a single-high safety with the receivers manned up underneath, there's a good chance you're seeing Cover 1. You can tell if it's man coverage by looking at the alignment of the pass defenders. If their eyes on locked on their assigned receiver, it's man. But, if they're tilted and looking at the quarterback, it's zone.

(BJ Smith)

Cover 2

The most common pass defense in football is Cover 2. What some coaches call "2-zone" because it's a pure zone coverage. It's your basic "bend-don't-break" defense. The two safeties at the top—what are commonly referred to as "2-high safeties"—are playing zone and so are the five defenders underneath them.

Short passes are hard to complete versus a 2-zone because the short areas are covered, but sending multiple receivers deep can tie up the safeties.

(Rusty Tanton)

The first clue that the coverage is 2-zone is the 2-high safeties. If they're positioned on the hashmarks, then that's a good sign they're splitting the deep end of the field into "halves."

The way to tell if the underneath coverage is playing zone is to look at their eyes. If they're on the quarterback, it's zone. But if they're on the receiver, it's man. The cornerbacks might be aligned "tight" on the receivers, and give the appearance of man coverage but at the snap of the ball, they can quickly transition into zone coverage.

Cover 2 is a fairly good defense against the run because everyone is looking into the backfield so they'll see a hand-off to a running back or the quarterback keeping the ball and running with it.

This scheme has the cornerbacks—the defensive farthest outside—cover the sidelines, while the outside linebackers are playing zone inside. Because they're so far out—"on an island," coaches call it—the cornerbacks have to be superb tacklers, especially in space, as they're relied on heavily in run support.

The two deep safeties, meanwhile, must have great speed because they're asked to cover a lot of "open grass," and their coverage skills must be above average. Good might get it done in high school but not in college or the pros.

But, by rushing four defensive linemen and dropping seven defenders into zone coverage, the Cover 2 scheme can eliminate most vertical routes while forcing the quarterback to throw the ball underneath the deep safeties or to a designated receiver who is running a *checkdown* route. The checkdown is simply a safe route that is easily thrown to a receiver that prevents the quarterback from being sacked. Like a *safety valve*.

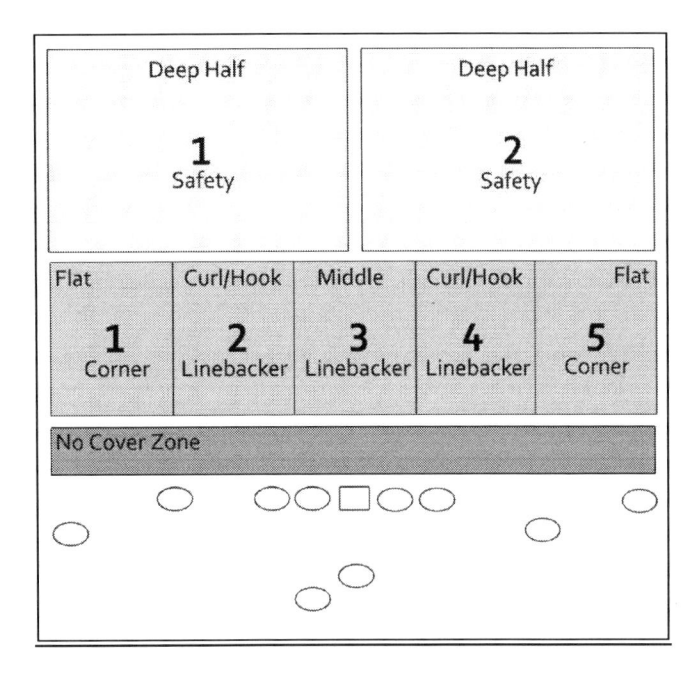

Cover 3

Cover 3 is another pure zone scheme. It positions three defenders deep and has four underneath. The three playing deep are generally a defense's best and fastest pass defenders: the two cornerbacks and the free safety. They split the deep end of the field into thirds, which is what most coaches call this supposedly high school defense: "Thirds."

(Robert Welch)

While the two cornerbacks and the free safety cover the deep end of the field, the strong safety drops down into the box to help with run support. When defending the pass, the strong safety and three linebackers drop into the four underneath zones, while the four defensive linemen pressure the quarterback.

The principal weakness of this defense is found near the sideline, in the flanks of the scheme. When the cornerbacks drop into deep coverage, the outside areas are exposed to short, quick throws. Its strengths, though, are that its three best pass defenders are playing deep, so long passes are covered. While underneath, the best tackler among the defensive backs—the strong safety—is up close to the offense and can get into the mix during a run play.

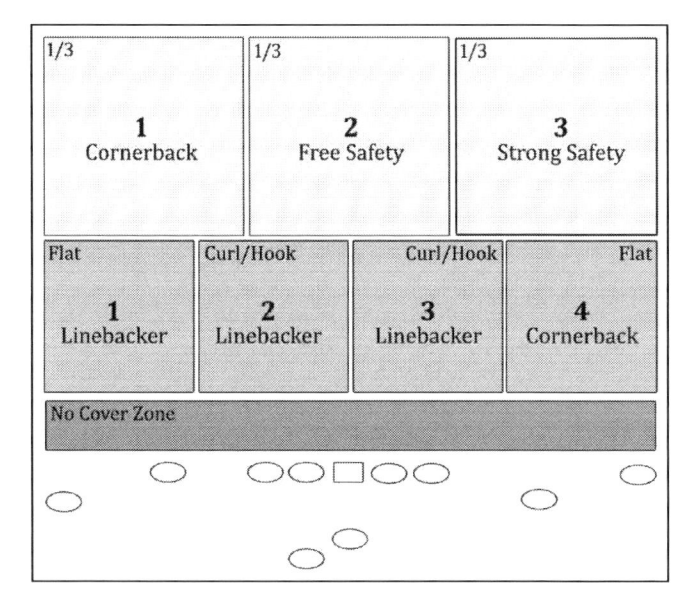

For a "high school" defense, Cover 3 isn't too shabby. In fact, the Seattle Seahawks won a Super Bowl using Cover 3. What they did is fix the hole in the scheme by having the cornerbacks align in "press coverage" on the outside receivers and jam them before backing off into their deep third of the field. This tactic took away the short pass to the outside.

It's not easy to tell if you're looking at a Cover 3 defense because it can easily start out looking like Cover 1, and often does. Three defenders aligned deep before the snap is a good indicator the scheme is Cover 3, but the cornerbacks aligned "off" the wide receivers is another, since they can quickly transition into a 3-deep look once the ball is snapped.

Often, too, the outside linebackers are positioned close, if not in the box, rather than opposite a receiver. The idea is to be close to provide run support, but the problem is that defense is then weak against the quick passes to the outside mentioned previously.

Cover 4

Better known as "quarters," Cover 4 sets four defenders deep. So little if anything is going to get past them, and it's great versus the run because everything is in front of them. The four deep defenders divide their end of the field into—you guessed it—quarters. It's sort of like Cover 3 flipped upside down, because the three linebackers divide the underneath area into "thirds."

(BJ Smith)

The weakness in the defense is the same area of the field as Cover 3 but unlike Cover 3, quarters coverage abandons the outside to the short pass. And the running attack. The thinking is that the deep defenders can quickly attack anything underneath. It's sort of like a Prevent defense in that it prevents anything, be a pass or a run, from going deep.

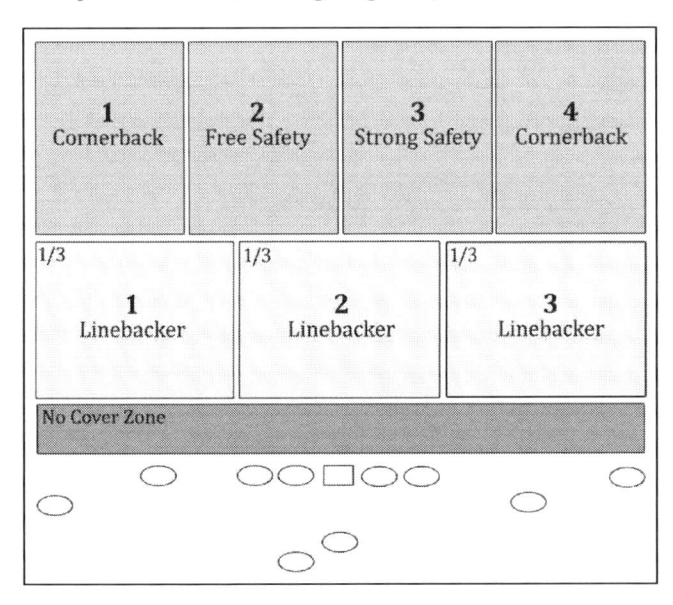

In most cases a quarters defense will start out looking like "2-Zone" (Cover 2) with two deep safeties. So look to the cornerbacks to check their depth. Again, as in "thirds," if they're playing off the receiver, that's a good indication they'll bail at the snap of the ball and drop into a fourth of the of field. Another indicator is the alignment of the outside linebackers. There's a good chance they'll be cheating to the outside to get in their zone quicker.

And everyone will be watching the quarterback.

Cover 5

Cover 5 is rarely called that. Its more common name is "2-Man" or "2-deep/man under," which describes the defense perfectly. It has two deep safeties playing zone like in Cover 2, but the five underneath defenders are manned up on the receivers.

When you see two deep defenders, just look to the underneath defenders to see if they're focused on the quarterback or the receiver opposite them. If the receiver, it's man coverage and you're looking at a "2-Man" defense.

(Rusty Tanton)

You'll see this defense a lot versus spread offenses because of the number of receivers they usually send downfield. It's great versus vertical passes—those that go deep—while pushing the short to intermediate routes. Often you'll see the cornerbacks playing "off" the wide receivers, but they're still manned up. They might peek into the backfield, but their primary focus will still be on the receiver.

What commonly happens when a receiver goes deep versus a 2-Man defense is that he picks up "double coverage" from the defender manned up on him and the safety whose zone he has entered.

Conclusion

These are the basics. The initial blueprints. Ingenious defensive coordinators can manipulate and add to their design, based on the skill and speed of their players. It doesn't help, either, that defenses are always disguising their attack with pre-snap alignments intended to confuse the quarterback's read. Then, at the snap of the ball, they quickly transition into something else entirely. That's why quarterbacks also have a *post-snap* read.

You may never figure it all out, but don't feel bad, as many coaches don't either. But knowing the basics will help you figure out enough that your understanding of the game will increase, and so will your enjoyment of it.

ADDENDUM TWO

Some Food for Thought...

I don't recall exactly when I started playing football. I just recall that when I did, the ball seemed bigger than me.

As I grew older and understood the game better, my father took me to Norman, OK and the football stadium there to watch the Oklahoma Sooners play. Afterward, we'd eat foot-long chili dogs, washed down by strawberry milk shakes and talk about the game.

(eBay)

It became a ritual of sorts, and I remember thinking as I watched Bud Wilkinson, the head coach, pace the sideline during the game that he had a great job.

(Santa Banta Forum)

Little did I know that one day I too would pace the sideline, but because of those trips to Norman with my father, I grew up dreaming of playing football for Oklahoma. Supporting the Sooners was, back then, a kind of religion my family practiced on Saturdays, especially if the Sooners were on TV.

We ate a lot of barbecue on those days, which left Sundays entirely to God and the long formal table around which we gathered and, after we prayed, partook of my Aunt Georgia's good food. Despite the variety of pies displayed on the kitchen counter, my Uncle Al would break up cornbread into a tall glass and pour milk over it, then eat it with a large spoon like it was pudding.

In the fall the talk among the men was mostly about the previous day's game. Sundays were a good day when the Sooners had won on Saturday, and back then Sundays were almost always good days.

(Tip Top 25)

Later, when I was in 8th grade and lived in Tacoma, WA, where I attended A. G. Hudtloff Junior High School, I was struck in the head by a football and

FOOTBALL FOR MOMS AND SWEETHEARTS

lapsed into a coma for 26 hours. My father told me that I almost died, but I was more upset when the doctors informed my dad that I couldn't play football for two years.

I loved the game, but I didn't know how much until 1978 when, more by circumstance than any initiative on my part, I was offered the head coaching job of the community's middle school team: the Heidelberg Panthers.

That's Heidelberg, Germany.

(Heidelberg University)

I was in the Army at the time, and I was the lowest ranking man on the staff, and yet I was the head coach. The world was upside down there for awhile, especially during practice. I had majors and warrant officers coaching for me, and I was just a sergeant.

I wasn't particularly talented. Just lucky. And mostly because I could draw upon the example set by my high school coach, Dick Luttrell, who I never heard raise his voice in anger.

For years I had avoided anything resembling a career by staying in the Army because I didn't know what else to do with myself. I could do what the Army asked of me standing on my head. But when it came to the real world, I didn't know what, if anything, I could be or do until the Friday walk-through practice we conducted before our first game with Karlsruhe.

The evening before—a Thursday—the father of our middle linebacker and I disassembled 40 helmets and painted each one gold. Once dried, we affixed an "H" to either side and two stripes down the middle, using black electrical tape. It took us all night.

(Nancy Proulx)

But the next day, when I saw those helmets lined up on the green grass of the practice field, followed by 40 beaming smiles, I knew instantly what I wanted to do. I knew I wanted to spend the remainder of my life recreating that look on the faces of other kids.

I knew I wanted to be a coach. And lucky me, I became that.

I tell you this not to boast, but so you'll know why I love the game—why I'm so inclined by sentimental notions and some nostalgia to defend it. I know it needs to be improved, and I have very specific ideas about how to accomplish that—mostly at the youth level and mostly with the coaching which is often poor to bad.

If you're son (or daughter) has a coach who doesn't know why a proper three-point stance is important or how to teach it, or—more importantly—doesn't know how to teach a proper form tackle, then your son (or daughter) needs a new coach—or a new team.

It's really that simple.

But the talk to abolish the game seems extreme and ill-considered. It would be a mistake, I think. Not because so many of us wouldn't know what do with our time on a fall weekend if football weren't being played, but because, like baseball, we grew up with the game.

And when you think about it, so did our country.

FOOTBALL FOR MOMS AND SWEETHEARTS

Football has been with us since after the Civil War, and it's ingrained into the national character. What is best about the game is also what is best about us. The qualities that make a player or a team great are the same qualities that make us uniquely American and make our country great.

But I'm a coach now and bigger than the ball, and the simple truth is that I love what football teaches young men about the bigger game called life. Of the many lessons the game teaches, the most important, I think, is the meaning of commitment, and not just to excellence on the field, but to excellence off it as well.

There is no excellence either on or off the field unless there is a commitment to the work, discipline, and sacrifice needed to achieve both personal and team goals. There's no success without a commitment to preparation and teammates. Especially when confronted with obstacles, adversity, and—at times—defeat.

In short. there has to be a commitment to give best effort in all things and to never give up. That one word, commitment, encompasses everything a player can acquire from the game, everything he can take with him off the field and into the classroom, into the workplace, or simply into life.

And while football isn't everything, I would argue that what a young man can—and will—learn about himself from playing the game, is. From this perspective then, I urge anyone who questions the value of football to look closely at the good that can come from the sport when it's properly taught.

But then I'm biased. A Friday night under the lights doesn't pass that I don't think about my dad and the chili dogs and strawberry milkshakes we shared.

Or that sometimes, in my sleep, I still dream of playing football for Oklahoma.

Coach G.

(touthouse)

Offensive Line
Silver Valley High School
Yermo-Fort Irwin, CA
2017

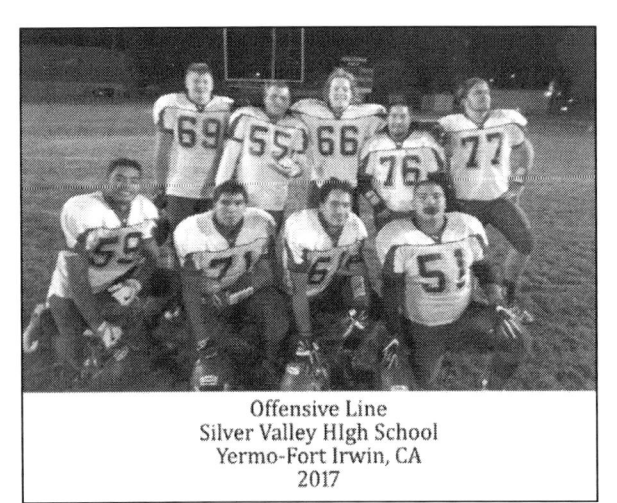

(Shawn Kittrel)

Made in the USA
San Bernardino, CA
03 November 2017